Building Respect, Responsibility & Spiritual Values in Your Child

Building Respect, Responsibility & Spiritual Values in Your Child

MIKE PHILLIPS

BETHANY HOUSE PUBLISHERS
Minneapolis, Minnesota 55438
A Division of Bethany Fellowship, Inc.

Published by Bethany House Publishers
A Division of Bethany Fellowship, Inc.
6820 Auto Club Road, Minneapolis, Minnesota 55438

Printed in the United States of America

Library of Congress Cataloging in Publication Data

Phillips, Mike, 1946-
    Building respect, responsibility, and spiritual
values in your children.

    Bibliography: p.
    1. Family—Religious life.   2. Christian
education of children.   I. Title.
BV1590.P44   649'.7   81-1225
ISBN 0-87123-146-8 (pbk.)   AACR2

Dedication

To Judy, whose joyful, frustrating, fulfilling, demanding and ever-deepening relationships with our three boys embody the principles in this book.

She has made a great commitment to them; it has required not only personal sacrifices and great love, but also exhausting amounts of time—and energy—daily. I marvel at her capacity to give so much of herself—to them and to me continually. Admittedly, she often gropes for answers to her daily dilemmas. But if you could *observe* her relationships (their strengths *and* faults) with our sons, I would scarcely need to *write* on this subject at all. I have merely written; she has made these principles LIVE! This book has been truly a joint effort.

The day will surely come when "her sons rise up and call her blessed." I want to add to their praise by affirming, "Many women have done excellently, but you surpass them all" (Prov. 31:28, 29).

Judy, I love you!

About the Author

MIKE PHILLIPS was raised in California, graduated from Humboldt State University, and had every intention of pursuing a career in physics or mathematics. But instead he got hooked on books. Beginning with a small, part-time selling effort in an upstairs apartment, he branched out and now heads One Way, Ltd., with Christian bookstores in northern California and Oregon as well as a small publishing company. He and Judy were married in 1971 and have three sons, Patrick, Gregory, and Robin. Judy does the accounting for the business and handles the active children. Home is Eureka, California, and the priorities of Mike's life, in addition to writing, are his family and the expanding bookstore ministry. He is the author of nine books, including the Bethany House publications *A Christian Family in Action* and *A Survival Guide for Tough Times.*

Contents

1. Mom and Dad, Do You Have a Plan?

There are hundreds of books on raising children. Even so, many Christian parents wander aimlessly through their child's early years trying to "do the best we can." Tragically, many later discover "the best we can" was not enough.

Most of us fall into the trap of thinking that common sense will somehow see us through. Simply because we *are* parents and have survived thus far (and possibly have already raised a child or two), we assume we are well-qualified to raise a child to maturity. But there's a big difference between keeping a roof over a child's head until he's eighteen and building godliness—respect, responsibility, and spiritual values—into him. Building godliness takes something more! Sadly, many parents miss this aspect of parenting altogether. But it doesn't have to be that way. You *can* be a successful parent and raise godly children. In this book we will uncover some principles that will make such an ideal a reality in your family.

If you are reading this book, it is probably because you *want* to build godliness into your child. That's an important first step—a *desire* for something greater than "average" for your son or daughter.

Children are like enormous sponges. Every waking moment they "soak up" all that is around them at a furious rate. They are also like lumps of pliable clay, waiting to be formed. As a parent, you are a potter—gently shaping, standing back to look, then continuing to shape that "clay" personality toward its envisioned design.

Both artists and builders work with clear plans before them. A sculptor with no design makes every cut haphazardly. A builder without an exacting set of blueprints constructs a house that is weak and unattractive. You also must have a design or a picture of what you want your child's character to be. What do you want to build into his life? Without *specific* plans, your work will have no purpose and your son or daughter will become something over which you exercised little control.

Planning is essential; successful parents must establish *specific* goals they intend for their child to reach. Regrettably, most parents are not daily setting imaginative goals and creating strategies for reaching them. We all *hope* our children will grow up walking with the Lord and we pray for God's help to be effective parents. But our own control over this process is something we haven't much considered.

Do YOU have specific goals for your child? Have you devised methods by which to achieve them? Many parents do not. And if you have, your goals and methods are no doubt hazy at best. But imagine a contractor trying to build houses with the same lack of planning. He would go bankrupt. A successful builder spends many hours thinking, drawing, calculating, projecting, and then re-drawing. He knows success is impossible without good planning. He is aware of Jesus' words, "For which of you, desiring to build a tower, does not first sit down and count the cost, whether he has enough to complete it?" (Luke 14:28).

Christian parents cannot do otherwise. God will call your child to be a mighty man or woman, to live and serve Him in uncertain times. He has given your child into your care for but a brief moment; you are to mold him into a person who will love and obey God at any cost.

Don't miss out on this tremendous calling! A great deal of your child's future rests with you. He is being shaped permanently, for all eternity, by *your* hands. You can mold him into any shape you choose. You *can* be a successful parent!

Within every youngster is magnificent potential, lying dormant, waiting to be drawn to the surface. Under your care and authority your child can realize his potential. This is possibly the most important task of your life. This requires a long-term vision and commitment. Naturally, you will have to sacrifice personal freedom as you devote time and energy to your child. But the stakes are high and the rewards for faithfulness are great.

In faith begin to visualize your child as God sees him— at the pinnacle of maturity. God does not merely see a child as he is at two, three, or seven, but *as a full-grown*, godly man or woman. He loves young children no less than adults. Yet God views each of us as what we are *becoming*, not simply as what we happen to be at some intermediate and incomplete stage. God always discerns the full, splendid potential lying hidden in each person, waiting to explode into life: "Before I formed you in the womb I knew you, and before you were born I consecrated you; I appointed you a prophet to the nations" (Jer. 1:5).

You must also "see" your child this way. For your child will ultimately grow to fulfill whatever vision you carry of him in your heart. If you want him to turn out a given way, *visualize* him that way. The "faith-pictures" you form will determine many of his lifetime characteristics. Therefore, don't allow your thinking to grow vague. Train yourself to say, "*This* is how I see my little Suzie thirty years from now!"

Wow, what a picture!

Vision is the key to successful parenting. Being a "decent parent" is not a sufficient goal. If a child, at seventeen or eighteen, suddenly doffs his seemingly good character and struts off to live his own way, his parents watch in stunned silence.

"Where did we go wrong?", they ask.

Like an unskilled sculptor, their work was piecemeal, consisting of fragmentary efforts—some good, some bad. There was no vision, no plan, no goal. *Though conception of children can occur unintentionally, effective parenting cannot!* Hit-and-miss tactics won't work. Goals and plans are essential.

Take some time right now and visualize your child in the future. What do you want him to be like? Do you see him sharing possessions, reading certain kinds of books, ministering to people, walking with God, devouring his Bible or serving God on the mission field? Be creative! *What do you see?*

Those mental images will become your goals. What you want your child to become, he *can* become. With that faith-portrait in your mind, you can set out to apply the principles set forth in this book and be on the way to achieving the end-product you desire: a godly child.

When I visualize my sons in the future, all sorts of desired qualities spring to my mind: wisdom, faith, confidence, courage, tenderness, self-control, trust, leadership, patience, kindness, endurance, humility, sensitivity, cheerfulness, thankfulness, etc. I think such distant faith-thoughts often. And from such imaginings emerge focused pictures of what I want to do as a parent. My mental faith-picture tells me what I should stress. For instance, knowing that a specific goal is to instill respect prepares me for teaching principles of respect in the proper situations. My mental picture of respectfulness forms the framework for what I actually do.

It is essential to spend a great amount of time visualizing by faith your children's futures. Those mental pictures will keep you on target.

2. Make a Commitment to Put Your Child First

It's much easier not to expend daily, moment-by-moment effort on raising your child. What do you do when Timmy gets angry with little sister Jeanne or when your thirteen-year-old wants to talk to you—and you have guests coming within the hour? What do you do on Friday evening when your tired feet and aching head drag you toward your easy chair but your sixteen-year-old has been waiting all week for help fixing his bicycle? Do you see these situations as opportunities to build toward your long-range goals for your child? Or do you hurry through, or even avoid these encounters, viewing them as interruptions?

Certainly it is more difficult to turn off the TV, remove the pan from the stove, or shut off the lawn mower in order to devote thirty minutes to your son or daughter. But such time spent in close interaction, instruction, and perhaps discipline or training of some kind can affect his or her life permanently. It's difficult to maintain that level of mental energy which views *every* interruption as important, but a meaningful and growing relationship requires such an attitude on your part.

Don't deceive yourself into thinking that just because

you are around your child, you are building character. You've got to expend effort.

A friend of mine wrote the following article for our church bulletin:

> My son turned to me the other day and said, "Dad, I don't think you spend enough time with me doing things I like to do." After a brief discussion, I resumed mowing the lawn. *Why can't he understand my pressures and growing responsibilities?* I thought.
>
> I really do try to spend time with my son, but I've been thinking a lot about his comment. I used to think that if I were home doing my chores (the lawn, the garden, the fences, changing oil in the car, etc.) that I would meet the needs of my children. I would do my projects and they could do theirs and, maybe through a mystical process, training would occur and all would be content.
>
> After several years of mowing lawns, planting gardens, fixing fences, and changing oil, I've come to the conclusion that mowing lawns, fixing fences, and changing oil is a sequence that is without end.
>
> My deeper conclusion is that my whirlwind home projects have really been excursions into my world of selfishness. My basic motivation has not really been the work at hand but, rather, to isolate myself from responsibilities to communicate with my wife and children.
>
> "Dad, I don't think you're spending enough time with me doing things I like to do." Translated, this is really, "Dad, I miss you. Dad, can I play with you? Dad, spend some time with me."*

No greater investment of time or energy can be made than devoting time to your child. Under Christ's lordship, your family *must* be preeminent above other interests, activities, and goals if you are going to raise a godly child. Make this decision in advance or your parental effective-

---

*Ron Wunner in *Gathered Together*, April 27, 1980. Used by permission.

ness will flounder. The forces pulling against your family are strong and steady. Only such a clear-cut priority will bring success.

Worldly executives are not the only ones who fail at this point; active, respected, and spiritual Christians also fail. You can easily miss the extreme importance of what the small moments of each day represent in the life of your child. Don't drift along from year-to-year merely assuming he will somehow assimilate your spiritual values from random bits and pieces he somehow acquires. Values and attitudes are not automatically conferred on one generation by its parents, and more importantly, neither is saving faith.

There are many biblical examples of parental failure. Eli was a dedicated servant of the Lord, but he failed as a father, and God severely judged him and his sons (1 Sam. 2:12-17:22-36; 3:11-14; 4:11-22).

Samuel was one of the finest examples of spiritual faithfulness in the Old Testament. He remained obedient to God throughout his life. Samuel had grown up in Eli's home. He had watched Eli lose his sons to the world. He knew the consequences of failure in fatherhood. He knew what Eli had done wrong and what mistakes he should have avoided. Samuel is a parallel of the man or woman who has read all the right books, who has parenting principles "down pat." And yet Samuel proceeded to fail as well—he lost his sons exactly as Eli had (1 Sam. 8:3).

Being a Christian, being a great leader, even being the most famous believer in the country (which is what Samuel was) is no guarantee of effectiveness as a parent.

The true test of your success as a parent will be the character of your future generations. Raising children who serve the Lord is good. But how much more impressive when a man's *grandchildren* reflect his values and convictions. The generation-to-generation progression holds the potential for you to influence thousands, perhaps millions. Make this the perspective of your efforts—to build godliness into future generations, to teach your sons and daughters to serve the Lord, *and* to teach their sons and daughters to do so.

But that will not happen just because you or I are Christians. If ever salvation and godly values could have been passed on in this "automatic" manner, it would surely have happened in Samuel's family. After all, he was a great man of God. But there is no automatic bestowal of salvation, there is no osmosis of godliness. Spiritual principles do not germinate in a child's heart without vigorous effort. You will have to make a HUGE investment in the young life of your child.

Eli and Samuel were too busy serving the Lord to build godliness into the lives of their sons. And it is possible for us, enlightened as we may be, to do the same. The years can quickly get away. With a breathless pace we pursue hobbies, cultivate friendships, improve our houses, solidify our careers, and involve ourselves more deeply at church. Many wives work so the family can have "more." Dads drag themselves home from work too tired to do anything but watch TV and maybe thumb through a magazine. The lists of projects and errands bombard parents continuously.

Pretty soon everyone is collapsing in bed after another hectic day. Suddenly it has been two weeks without significant communication between Dad and his growing, impressionable son. Mom has been too busy for five days to read to her wide-eyed four-year-old. Another day has passed when six-year-old Janie has played solitaire with her dolls; she desperately wants the company of her mother, even for ten minutes, but knows from past experience that her request will only be met with, "I'm sorry, dear, I'm busy. I've got dinner on the stove, and. . ."

Another day has passed with eight-year-old Tommy playing racquet ball against the fence in the back alley, aching for just a half-hour of his dad's company. But Dad's not home and poor Tom knows he won't be until after dark. So he spends another afternoon listlessly bouncing the ball, dreaming of the day last month when he and Dad played at the tennis court and the whole block rang with his laughter.

The days fade into weeks, then years. All of a sudden (or so it seems) ten or twenty years are gone. The kids are at college. The career ambitions so relentlessly pursued have lost their glimmer. The family room seems hollow. The ping-pong table is quiet. The sandbox is overgrown with weeds. The swing-set is rusty and still. We search the shadows of our memories to relive those precious experiences that we foolishly allowed to sweep by so quickly. The children's laughter rings in our ears. As we look deep into those faces so vividly projected within our memories, a mist comes to our eyes.

Now we can see; now it's so plain that those eyes were filled with the ache of unmet needs. How desperately they wanted *us*. And how much more we could have given. But we were too busy. And the pleading in their faces wasn't as clear then as it now seems to be.

Without a priority commitment *now*, such memories will haunt us. And we may one day wake to discover that we too are on that same parental path that Samuel and Eli trod long ago. The world's system opposes nearly every value you would like implanted in your child. Satan is battling furiously for his heart, mind, and soul. He will deceive him at every opportunity. You cannot possibly counter this awesome influence if you are too busy, tired, or distracted to play with, read to, listen to, teach, and pour yourself into your child. No amount of material success will compensate for depriving him of *yourself*. The exposure of your heart and character to him—for hours, days, and years—will affect his character more than anything else in his life.

This demands TIME. Time that you will not have to give if you are busy with your own pursuits and ambitions.

You must establish in your heart a commitment of time. Such a commitment can never be carried out from some lofty height of resolution. A promise of "I'll do better this year" on New Year's Eve will not cure your ineffectiveness as a parent. Rather, it's a commitment you will have to make a dozen times a day. Every time you face the choice to take time with your child, or to let the moment pass, you add something to his character—something positive or negative. Over the years, through the thousands of such choices you make—to either work into his life something of yourself or idealistically wait for "next time"—you will bit-by-bit build godliness into his character, or else allow the world to mold him into whatever it desires.

No moment you spend with your child is insignificant. That's what makes the commitment so important and so hard to make. It would be much simpler if you could, in a sweeping act of decision, determine to once-and-for-all be a great parent. But godly influence never happens quite so readily. Rather it hinges on each tiny moment of life. In those seconds and minutes you are building a personality for all eternity. The greatest calling you as a parent have will be fulfilled by what you do *in the next five minutes*—all your life-long.

By making that choice—to spend time building godliness into your child—you will be able at some future time to say to God, "Lord, here is my child. The work you gave me to accomplish in his life has been completed. He is now ready to serve you and I offer him back to you."

3. Your Child's Most Important Teacher: YOU

The human brain is more sophisticated than any computer man will ever devise. Scientists estimate that the brain attains half of its maximum capacity by the age of four, three-fourths by the age of eight. But like man-made computers, the brain must be programmed. As a parent, *you* are primarily responsible for the input your child's brain needs in those early years—*you* are the computer programmer. All children, from the moment of birth, have an instinctive hunger to learn. They chase knowledge furiously! And with the guidance and the motivation you supply, yours will learn faster and keep learning longer.

The universe is your classroom. It is yours to experience and yours to use as you introduce your child to all that God has to offer. The more diverse your teaching the more abundant your child's life can become.

Curiosity and Imagination—Roots of the Learning and Creativity Cycles

Learning begins with curiosity, which every toddler possesses in abundance. Children want to explore, touch, play with, and know about *everything* within reach of their senses. They are driven to learn by degrees of motivation they never will possess again in their lives. This period is your priceless opportunity to establish the direction and momentum of your child's learning.

Curiosity breeds discovery. Children see something and are curious. They move to explore it—to touch, taste, investigate. When in such exploration they make new discoveries, learning has taken place. Children learn as they repeat this simple process over and over again, thus reinforcing what they have discovered. Even without parents' help, children's learning rates are phenomenal because their curiosities never tire.

Many parents block this learning process with a constant barrage of, "No, no, don't touch." If children aren't allowed to complete this cycle of satisfying their curiosity through exploration and discovery, they are deprived of much they need to learn.

As they mature and as their skills solidify, children's capabilities and curiosities blend by degrees into creativity. When creativities begin to blossom, the children are approaching a time when more direct guidance and stimulation will be required. Much of their earlier learning-through-exploration, if coupled with the confidence gained from parental encouragement, will be revealed as they begin to do and make things creatively. They will bring into reality pictures and projects they have dreamed up in their own minds.

This new behavior involves a three-step creative process. First, the child imagines something, perhaps a picture to draw or a structure to build. He then goes about "creating" what at first was only in his imagination—he draws the picture or builds the tower. Then after his creation is completed, he furthers his sense of accomplishment by holding the "masterpiece" in his hand and saying, "I can make something all by myself."

Both of these processes—learning and creativity—are constantly taking place in your child's mind. Curiosity leads to exploration which results in discovery. Imagination leads to creativity which results in accomplishment. As a parent you are in a position to insure that both processes are nurtured and directed.

You can stimulate your child's learning by participating in these processes with him and by providing ample resources to spark his curiosity and imagination. The alternative is to insensitively block both cycles and hinder his learning and inner growth. Children have enormous inborn drives, energies, and curiosities. But soil in which the same crops are planted year after year eventually become exhausted. Likewise, children's natural hunger for learning can dissipate. Without steady nurturing, inquisitiveness and imagination will decline. But with guidance from parents who awaken them in ever new directions, these qualities will develop throughout their lives.

In order to become a well-rounded and creative adult, a child must have stimulating early years. Your job is to provide an environment in which yours can learn, create, question, explore, and expand. The more experiences he has, the larger will be his sphere of understanding and expression. He needs outings to the zoo, dairy, park, woods, beach, stores, construction projects, etc. And you can provide other experiences right at home through books, kitchen projects, and backyard activities. Almost anything can offer food for the creative mind.

It has been theorized that nearly every child is born with the mental capability for genius. Only insufficient stimulation prevents the genius from emerging.

As a youngster wonders at new discoveries and devises new attempts to create, his mind becomes even more inventive. *Creativity feeds itself.* Every new idea he uncovers makes him more capable of thinking on his own.

Creativity and Learning

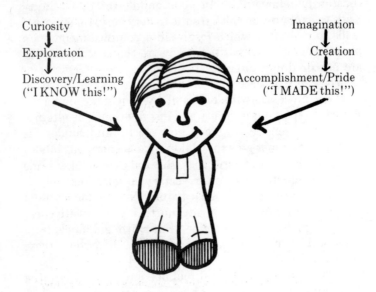

Curiosity
↓
Exploration
↓
Discovery/Learning
("I KNOW this!")

Imagination
↓
Creation
↓
Accomplishment/Pride
("I MADE this!")

The result: a well-rounded, capable, knowledgeable, imaginative, creative adult

Every child has been blessed by God with the gift of imagination. But in some it never grows. It is a fragile sprout, easily crushed if trampled by a lumbering parent too busy to get down on his hands and knees to view life from the fresh perspective of his son or daughter. Yet within an atmosphere of freedom, imagination is nourished and grows boundlessly.

You enlarge his imagination still further by exploring life *with* your child. If you can excercise an imagination that makes even the minor things in life exciting, his own creative juices will flow faster. But if when he sees faces in the clouds, becomes intoxicated with Santa Claus, or relishes his make-believe world, you continually smother his enthusiasm, you will cut him off from worlds that might otherwise be his. Yet as you reveal to him the unusual, ask questions, put visions inside his head, point out life's oddities, read to him, and listen to his ideas, you will encourage a productive mind.

Marguerite Kelly and Elia S. Parsons write:

> Everyone is born with imagination, but no flower in the soul of man is more easily crushed—or more easily nourished. You nurture this imagination when you let your child explore, when you trust in his ability—to climb a tree, to create a song, to dress up like a king and to simply sit and dream. In these ways, you're giving him the right to think for himself.
>
> Your own inventiveness can stretch his imagination. The questions you ask, the fancies you suggest, the problems you pose, all put visions in his head. When you encourage your child to substitute the unusual for the obvious—a rock for a hammer, a can of beans for a rolling pin, a different mug instead of his favorite—you're stirring his imagination too. . . .
>
> The child who is asked to shut his eyes and listen hard enough to describe every sound he hears—the blue jay and the diesel brakes; the drier tumbling clothes; scissors clicking—will not only have a better awareness of sounds but a richer reservoir of words, for he becomes more conscious of them. Each time he's pushed to be clever with words, he can express himself better and he can think better too.[1]

Curiosity and imagination stretch the capacity of the mind to probe areas that might otherwise remain untouched. A mind that probes the unusual, the new, the unknown is a mind more able to understand the self and to explore the hidden reaches of God's world, His principles and His infinite character. Without a vibrant imagination and curiosity, a person is only partially developed; without it, it is impossible to fulfill the command: "You shall love the Lord your God with all your heart, and with all your soul, and with *all your mind*" (Matt. 22:37).

Self-discovery

In the process of discovering, learning occurs. You cannot discover *for* your child, but you can provide an environment rich with potential discoveries. Take him places where he can experience what would be impossible at home. Let him sit in the seat of a fire engine, pet a cow, feed a duck. A variety of books can help accomplish the same purpose. Provide ample "things" to play with when he is young: blocks, paints, tools, crayons, old magazines, scissors, cardboard boxes, glue, and "dress-up" clothes. For a toddler or preschooler, these are the raw materials of his curriculum. They provide substance for creative activity. They lead to discoveries large and small. Future abstract thinking will be enhanced by such early concrete experience.

Creativity is not static but is constantly changing and evolving. Just because a particular child is not a gifted artist or musician does not mean he has no creativity. As a parent you must recognize how to "draw out" your child's gifts, interests, and the unique aspects of his own personality.

Creativity is the ability to bring something to reality out of nothing. This definition provides much latitude; multiplying money through childhood projects, soothing anger between playmates, making friends, cooking, and nailing together wood scraps are *all* reflections of creativity. God created each child with different gifts and desires. Our job as parents is to nurture those unique traits and draw that creativity out from *wherever it lies*. Maybe your son makes the biggest, messiest mudpies on the block. That is creativity!

Your child should be able to enter school with his head high, with the assurance that "I am a creative person!" It's up to you to build that positive attitude.

It is vital for a youngster to make discoveries and draw conclusions *on his own*. It's hard as parents to stand back; we always want to say, "Blue and yellow make green." But how much more significant to simply offer the paints and wait—maybe two days, maybe a month—until that exciting moment when we hear from the next room, "Hey, I mixed blue and yellow and they turned to green!"

Children must know why and how things work. That is how they learn. They *will* make discoveries if you allow them to. Toys can stimulate or stifle this process. If a toy requires creativity it is a good one. For example, a cardboard box large enough to get inside can be used as a playhouse, a car, an airplane, a cave, or a bed. Each different application of the box stimulates the imagination. Thus, some of the best toys do not come from the toy store at all. However, building blocks and the many varieties of "construct-o-gadgets" are also flexible enough to allow creativity.

Contrast those with a battery-operated toy in which 95% of the play comes from the mechanics of the toy itself, leaving little room for the child's imagination to work. The more a toy does *for* the child, the less he uses it to develop his creativity. I expect that the new wave of computer toys will, in a few years, have contributed to a drastic decline of creative abilities in young school-children, in much the same way that television already has.

The Increasing Need for Direct Verbal Teaching

When a child's understanding expands, he will begin to

question and search for answers that his own exploration cannot provide. Your teaching must then become increasingly straightforward. He will need more and more of your direct input.

Your most effective teaching method at such times, however, will not be lecturing, but interaction, which will require much attentiveness on your part. Gradually you will feed your child information about life, God, tractors, weather, relationships, plants, toys, school, money, geography, animals, death—the lists will be different for each age. Through the endless daily small-talk, you will shape his outlook on life. But to be dynamic and effective, this ongoing dialogue must flow *both* ways—you must transmit concepts *to* him and at the same time receive *from* him his questions and responses.

Often insignificant daily tasks provide the best teaching opportunities—a fix-up job, a bit of weeding, a run to the grocery store, or painting the new fence. The wise parent adds a few minutes to the job, includes his child from start to finish and teaches along the way. Sharing life in this manner not only passes along fundamental skills, it builds confidence and strengthens your relationship. The atmosphere must be relaxed; a child cannot be forced to learn. But when you provide such situations where learning is possible and treat your child as a capable and helpful individual, he will learn—and will love it.

Our household is incredibly vocal. We talk to our boys about *everything*. There is pressure from the constant talk that we as parents cannot help but sometimes feel—the unending questions, explanations, and interruptions can be nerve-racking. The high level of attentiveness required can be maddening at times. Yet this intense, wordy interchange is the essence of a parent-child teaching relationship. You can, of course, avoid the stress of interaction by sending your child off to play in the family room. You may indeed achieve some peace and quiet but you will be losing a valuable opportunity to build his young life—an opportunity you will never have again.

It is easy to view such continuous "trivial" conversations as interruptions to other projects and duties. A father may halfheartedly carry on a conversation with Junior, but his thoughts are really on watching the football game or planning tomorrow's crucial interview. He only responds passively. The child must initiate every discussion, every question. Dad only answers back as necessary. He makes no conscious attempt to build his son's life.

Certainly there are urgent concerns on your daily agenda. But the vigorous teaching that deeply influences a youngster's life is accomplished at a heavy personal price. Therefore, I try (with varying degrees of success) to focus intently on every conversation I am having with one of my boys; I block out thoughts of my overdue bills at the store or the problems at my church or the friend I am counseling. At that particular moment *they* are the intrusion and my son is the center of attention. Those small discussions about the skinned elbow, the wobbly bicycle wheel, the difference between Jesus and God, and the broken toy are the building blocks for a future of intimacy as well as the foundation for my relationship with him as his teacher.

Children desperately long to fill every corner of their minds. An attitude which reserves more of our quiet moments for ourselves is not God's pattern for us as parents. This doesn't mean you organize and prepare in advance lessons to reel off while your child takes notes. Such schoolroom teaching would doom your attempt from the beginning. Instead, I let my boys determine the pace and direction of their "lessons." I grab the openings as they come.

Exposure to many aspects of life will prompt a child to ask many questions, as unpredictable in content as they are in timing. But when a child thus opens the door to his mind, be ready. A question indicates a supreme moment for the sensitive parent to teach the receptive child. In that moment the child is wide open. The wise parent must be ready with a thoughtful response. Your child's unfathomable curiosity is one of your great allies in this teaching process.

Many parents sidestep or even disregard questions posed by their youngsters—as if such questions were an annoying distraction from the major concerns of life. Not me! I love the questions! I don't dodge them; I handle every one, encouraging even more questions. I use them as springboards to discussion.

I know that my boys' early years provide my greatest opportunities for this. Those mental doors may not always be open. If I don't enter in to teach and mold them in those years when they are most pliable, *others* will. Someone will teach my sons—their hungry minds will see to that. And if I do not "feed" them, they will seek "food" elsewhere.

You are the one responsible to show your child the world, to teach him about God's love, to stimulate and draw out his creative abilities. You have hundreds of opportunities to expand his horizons. Every day I talk to my boys about such things as snails, song lyrics, buds on the fruit trees, electrical substations, how big God is, how rain and clouds and evaporation work, pile-drivers, taking Mama out to dinner, how Santa Claus is a "type" of Jesus, the significance of church, what the Bible tells us to do, showing respect to old people, how to honor our spiritual leaders, where Walter Cronkite lives, driftwood on the beach, and thousands of other things. *Every* moment is jammed with potential!

Your child's mind is not stiff, but amazingly flexible. In fact, the farther you stretch it the greater its capacity to stretch even farther. Each activity, adventure, and conversation gives his imagination and intelligence a pull and takes him just a little farther beyond himself. Kelly and Parsons note:

> Every mind-stirring thing he meets will add to his wonder, which is as it should be. The more a child wonders, the more inventive and resilient his mind will be. Each new idea will make him more capable of thinking for himself, of exploring his own head for answers. At this age, he'll look at life from the underside, not only finding the unusual but expecting it: a viewpoint to be encouraged for the rest of his life.[2]

Every time you get down in the grass with your child to watch where the sow bug went, or warn him that there'll probably be rain tomorrow because of the change in the wind, or try to watch where the honey bees go to deposit their pollen, you'll be filling him with an excited, "What's next?" view of life. It will carry him on its crest as long as he lives. You'll not only enable him to see the world, its beauty, and its mystery, you'll also expand his capacity to comprehend something of God's magnificent love and creativity.

The Bulldozer, the Ditchdigger, and the Park

Attitudes, ideas, facts, and values are implanted in bite-sized pieces. As you expose your child to the world, simply allow the natural flow of events to open him up so that you can reveal your perspectives. This type of communication is much more effective than that of passing along specific data (even though that is important). Your character and the bond of love and trust you build at such times will have far greater impact than the words you say on any given day.

For example, one of the greatest times for me with my boys is in the late afternoon, just before dinner. Even the most ordinary day can be transformed into a momentous teaching occasion. Sometimes I come home at 3:30 or 4:00 and walk through the door calling, "Who'd like to go for a ride?"

There is instant commotion as Gregory, Robin, and Patrick scurry about to retrieve shoes, hats, and jackets. Before long we have all piled in the car, leaving Judy with an hour of *quiet* in which to fix dinner. Often I drive until we find a new building site. There's always some road-patching, sewer pipe installation, or apartment house project to be found nearby. If we make it in time to see the men still operating their equipment, so much the better. We then find a spot where we can sit down together and watch and discuss what is going on. A conversation like the following would not be unusual.

"Look at that deep hole. See the man way down inside it?"

"Why's he there, Daddy?"

"He's laying those big pipes in place. See that stack of them over there?"

"Why do they have to put pipes in the hole?"

"There are a lot of new houses being built near here. See that field over there? That's going to be a new subdivision."

"What's a subdivision?"

"It's a place where they build lots of new houses all close together. Those men are running a sewer line to those new houses."

"What does a sewer line do?"

"Well, all the water the people will use in those houses will drain out through the pipes—oh, oh, watch out! Here comes the bulldozer. Let's move back a little!"

"What's he going to do?"

"It looks like he's going to push that pile of gravel back into the hole on top of the pipe they've already laid."

"It sure is complicated, huh, Dad—just to lay a pipe in the ground?"

"Yes, it is."

"Wow! Look at the huge load that ditchdigger just picked up!"

"Where did that full dump truck take the last load?"

"Probably to some landfill where they needed the dirt."

On and on the banter might go as we watch the equipment and men and listen to the sounds and talk about what is happening around us.

If we are late in the day and the men have already left, we might take a closer look, both at the equipment and the hole.

"Hey, Daddy, look at me! I'm standing right at the edge of the hole the ditchdigger made."

"Deep, isn't it?"

"I'll bet it's over your head! Hey, look at Gregory trying to get up into that bulldozer!"

"Let me lift you up. Look, Robin, Patrick, here's Gregory the bulldozer man! Okay, dump some gravel in here."

"Here I go. Better stand back, Daddy. B-u-u-r-r-m-m!"

"Patrick, what are you doing?"

"I'm the ditchdigger man. I'm going to dig a hole for this pipe."

"Robin! Are you going to steamroll the new road?"

"Here comes the steamroller!"

After we are all through playing we may sit down and talk. The play has set the stage for openness. The discussion in the next ten minutes can go in a hundred different directions.

Other times we go to the park and walk through the woods, pretending to explore some distant land.

"Hey, look at this walking stick I found."

"Why don't you lead us for a while. Shall we call you Bilbo?"

"Yes, I'm Bilbo. Here we go to Gollum's cave!"

"Hey, Dad, what's this funny thing?"

"That's called a toadstool."

We all crouch down on our hands and knees and look. "It looks like a mushroom but it's poisonous, so don't ever eat something that looks like that."

"What's that funny smell?"

"I think it's skunk cabbage."

"Do skunks eat skunk cabbage?"

"I don't think so, Gregory. I don't even think there are any skunks around here. I think they call it skunk cabbage just because it has such a strong smell."

"Why did God make skunk cabbage, Dad?"

"I don't know, Patrick. He's so big and creative. He made many things we don't understand the purpose of."

"Like toadstools?"

"Are they called toadstools because toads sit on them?"

"That's a good one, Robin! I imagine that's just a name for them. And yes, Patrick. I don't know why God made toadstools either. But I do know that everything He made comes from His heart of goodness and love. So there must be a purpose for even toadstools—and skunk cabbage."

"Wow, what a pretty flower!"

"It's called a trillium. It's very delicate—try not to touch it."

"Why doesn't it have a smell?"

"It's just pretty like it is. God didn't make all flowers for the same reason."

"What a pretty place, huh, with the ferns and logs and stream and stumps?"

"Hey, look at that good stump there. Let's go climb it!"

"Look at me. I'm on top of the chimney, like Bert the Chimneysweep!"

"Whoooo! There's a *huge* stump. That's *too* big for us to climb. That's a stump for God to climb."

"I guess so, Gregory."

"How can God be so big, Daddy?"

"I don't know. I just know He's big enough to love and care for the whole world."

"Daddy, who made God?"

The conversation and questions continue unabated. From toadstools, skunk cabbage, and stumps, our talk may move to trees, the moon and sky, the wild animals, and from there to God's imagination for creating such a beautiful world. Rather than passively hauling my boys someplace and then lying around while they play, I seize these marvelous opportunities and energetically involve myself in their thoughts.

As yeast is kneaded deep into bread dough, so I work the experience of the construction site and the walk in the woods deep into their impressionable minds; my responses and questions insure that something greater than the bulldozer and the stumps is being processed in their minds. As we talk and romp together, I constantly feed bits of information, reflect aloud on their questions, and share my impressions. I enhance my words by allowing the boys to witness my moods; if feelings rise within me I don't squelch them; if thanksgiving to God overwhelms me, I don't hide it. In all this I give my boys glimpses of how I look at life and the world.

> It's the time you spend. . . and the way you spend it that determine the richness of the heritage. The summer walks may seem a bother, the fishing trip too much, but they set the mood for talking—a habit once set that can never be lost.[3]

My wife and I believe that everything that we discuss and everything that we see offers the potential for such give-and-take. We don't discourse on the meaning of life every five minutes. A rambunctious youngster couldn't tolerate that. But we faithfully "feed" pieces here, pieces there so that every conversation contributes to the view of life we desire our sons to possess.

Our use of the small moments of every day reveals much about our priorities. Our priorities will have lifelong impact on our children's perspectives of life. They remember those little moments of interaction (the first time Daddy played hide-and-seek with them, the morning Mommy took time out to make a Peter Pan or Johnny Appleseed costume, the evening Dad proudly showed the family Junior's earliest effort to trace a picture) far more than new toys or allowance bonuses.

Joyce Landorf recalls this incident from her own childhood:

> One of the most precious things my mother developed in me was the sense of wonder.
>
> I guess all children are born with a sense of wonder, but to reach adulthood with it intact and fully matured is practically a miracle.
>
> I was only a second- or third-grader when I first noticed a field of yellow dandelions while on my way home from school one day. I waded into that glorious golden sea of sunshine, picked all the blossoms my hands could hold, and ran all the way home. I flung the door open wide and shouted, "Here, Mother, these are for you!"
>
> At that moment, my mother was engaged in a Bible study with a roomful of ladies from our church. She had two options: shush me up, or develop my sense of wonder.
>
> In slow magnificent awe she laid her books on the table, knelt beside me, and took my gift.
>
> "Oh, they are beautiful, beautiful, beautiful," she said over and over again. (She could have told me they were messy weeds.) "I love them because you gave them to me." (She could have given me a lecture on picking flowers on private property.) "I'm going to set them on our table for our centerpiece tonight." (She could have told me they'd never last the afternoon and aside from drooping would make my father sneeze.)[4]

Implanting Spiritual Perspectives

Children do not accidentally inherit a spiritual value system; it must be deliberately ingrained in them. If you want your child to know and live out God's truths—His love, His provision, His power, and His commands—then you must tell him those principles and then *demonstrate* them in your life. Such concepts will not just "seep" into his mental framework of themselves.

In his pre-teen years, even the child most likely to turn from God may exhibit what appears to be a "close walk with the Lord." Parents can be lulled into a false confidence regarding his spirituality. Then when the teen years arrive, reality crashes in like a 747, and the parents realize they did not provide their child with strong *examples.*

Young people are not deceived by rote spirituality. When parents lack a solid trust in God and fail to practice His ways in life's details, their children's lives and attitudes will ultimately betray those inconsistencies, no matter how angelic the children may have appeared. Therefore you must do far more than simply *tell* your child about God and the church. You must do more than read the Bible and pray daily. *You must be the example of Jesus Christ in your home.* The verbal truths of obedience, prayer, respect, faith, and compassion will come to life for your child as he witnesses them in your life. What do they hear you say and see you do when the board slips and smashes your toe, when a store clerk is rude to you, or when the neighbor's dog tears up your garden?

As a parent you are on the job day and night, shaping your child's perspectives according to your own. If your actions line up with those things you have told him, he will accept what you tell him as reasonable. He will be secure in your consistency and will be all the more likely to accept your system of values fully as his own. But if he hears you say one set of things and sees you act contrary to your statements in a moment of stress, he will notice the inconsistency and his own life will eventually reflect it.

If I tell my son, "You should love every person, even the bully who picks on you at school," but continually mutter and growl about the "stupid neighbor" who lets his trash blow on our lawn, my son has good reason to suspect that I have a hole in my logic.

If I tell him, "God protects us and meets our every need," yet am constantly worrying about our bills and the effect of inflation upon our income, he has a legitimate right to question how practical God's protection and care really are in my own life.

Teaching must be far more than "lectures" or daily family devotions. Without a consistent example undergirding those activities, spiritual words will do more harm than good. If your practical example is shaky, your child will grow up mocking your words.

There are four essential steps in the process of effectively implanting spiritual truths in your child's heart:

1. *Information*—telling him a principle.

2. *Mental Application*—telling him how it applies to his life.

3. *Practical Application*—showing him how to apply it and helping him to do so.

4. *Example*—letting him see the principle applied in your life.

For instance, you may be trying to teach your daughter that God's people are to ease the burdens of people in need.

You might proceed as follows.

Step one—tell your daughter the principle.

"Honey, I'd like to discuss something with you."

"Sure, Mom, what is it?"

"God tells us that one of our responsibilities is to ease the burdens of those around us, to feel their hurts with them, to help meet their needs however and whenever we can. We are to sacrifice for the sake of someone else who is

having a difficult time, just as Jesus would do if He were
you or me. I've been watching you and I see that you already do this in many ways. Now I want you to gain a better
understanding of this principle."

You have now given her the information.

Step two—apply the truth to her own life.

"Let me give you an example of what I mean. Do you remember your youth group's weekend camping trip at the
lake last month?"

"Yes, what about it?"

"Do you recall why Sharon didn't go?"

"She couldn't afford the ten dollars for gas and food."

"What did the others do when they found out she wasn't
able to go along?"

"Oh, no one really said much about it. I guess nobody
cared that much."

"Sharon's kind of on the fringe of the group, isn't she?"

"She's a little—well, you know—younger than the rest
of us, and kind of, well, not really very pretty. Sometimes
some of the older girls make fun of her. I don't like it."

"I'm glad you don't like it. You're not supposed to.
That's not the way God wants us to treat people. You're a
sensitive girl and it's good you notice things like that. Do
you think Jesus would have treated His playmates like that
when He was a boy?"

"I doubt it."

"I don't think so either. Don't ever feel ashamed for no-
ticing when someone is being treated badly. We're supposed to notice and help that person if we can."

"But I just don't know what to do for Sharon. She's kind
of hard to talk to and when she does come to activities she
hardly says anything—she just keeps to herself."

"Do you know anything about her family?"

"I guess her dad's out of work and she has some younger

brothers and sisters. They live in a small house over on the other side of town. I've heard that they have kind of a hard time."

"You're right. Sharon is quiet and reserved because she's insecure about herself. She doesn't have much money and her folks can't afford nice clothes like the other girls wear. Don't you think she probably feels a little embarrassed, maybe inferior?"

"I never thought of that. She probably does."

"What do you think Jesus would do if He were at your activities and Sharon walked in? Do you think He'd care about being accepted by the in-group or do you think He'd care more about accepting Sharon?"

"I guess He'd care more about Sharon."

"You see, there's a situation where you could put that principle of easing another's burden into practice. Maybe next time she's in a group and you are there, you could follow Jesus' example and make her feel welcome and accepted—just by being her friend. It'll be hard, but just think what it will mean to Sharon to have someone care so much. And the Bible says that when God's people love others, in spite of what anyone else thinks, He will bless them."

Now you have not only presented the principle, you have applied it in a real-life situation. The more such applications you can make the more she will begin to sense the reality of the truth you have been discussing.

Step three—move her from mental understanding to *practical application*. At this point the principle can rise to life within your daughter. A Christ-like life comes from *practice* not knowledge. Now your daughter needs you as her skilled guide to take her hand and show her *how* to put the truth to work.

Several months later your daughter's youth group is planning another outing, this time to the city for a day of sight-seeing. Afterward they will "camp out" in a sister church and return home in the morning. The cost for this trip is fifteen dollars, which will cover a boat ride, meals, and gas.

As your daughter excitedly tells you about the plans, the wheels of your mind begin to turn.

"Hey," you suggest, "I've got an idea."

"What?" she asks.

"Since they need some drivers, would you like me to go along? Dad has to be out of town on business then anyway."

"That'd be great! Could I ride with you?"

"Sure. Anyone else you'd like to take in our car?"

"Oh, yeah. I'll ask Cindy and Marcia and—hey, Mom, what about Sharon? Do you suppose she'd want to come?"

"Great idea, honey!"

"The money, though, would be a problem. If she couldn't afford the ten dollars, then fifteen's going to be even worse."

"How are you planning to get your money?"

"I've got seven dollars saved up from my allowance and I was thinking about doing some yard work for the neighbors to earn the other eight."

"Why don't you and Sharon work on it together? Maybe we could have her over for dinner next week, and we could all brainstorm about how you and she could both earn enough money."

"That sounds neat. I know she'd love it."

"She could ride with us and we could really make an effort to make sure she felt included and had fun. It might really be a breakthrough for her. I think you and I working together could make her feel good about herself—because she's really a nice girl. I'd like to get to know her better."

"Oh, Mom, that's so neat of you. I'm excited already!"

Step four—line up your life with your words.

Obviously, such great lessons will not always be learned in three brief conversations. Such things will have to be part of the warp and woof of your family relationships. As she sees *you* giving extra attention to Sharon on the trip, inviting Sharon's mother to church and swapping recipes with her, as she sees your husband helping Sharon's father build a fence around his yard or possibly sending him an anonymous seventy-five dollars when times are tight, *then* she will see the reality of what you have been saying. She must see you relate to your own peers, friends, and business associates. Without your visible example, all your previous groundwork will have been in vain.

Our society is deep in moral decay. Christian parents must aggressively fulfill their God-given responsibilities to direct and teach their sons and daughters. Everything you desire to materialize in your child you must *teach and live.* Larry Christenson challenges:

> Be that yourself which you would bring others to be. Be it with your whole being. If your demands stand in contradiction to that which you yourself are in secret, then expect no success, no blessing. Expect, instead, that your work as a parent will be brought to shame.[5]

Do you want your child to be a man or woman of prayer? Then you will have to instruct him, practice with him, and show him. If your son is beaten up by some older boys on the way home from school, his natural response will not be to pray for them. You must lead him, getting down on your knees *with* him to pray for those boys.

He also must sense that prayer forms the foundation for everything *you* do. What is *your* reaction when you've been bilked in a business deal? Do you pray for those who have despitefully used you? He will want to know. His prayer life will be based on what he observes in your prayer life.

Do you want your child to daily seek for life's answers in God's Word? Do you want him to be able to hear God's voice speaking to and guiding him? Do you want him to rec-

ognize Satan's lies in the philosophies of the world? Do you
want him to victoriously battle against the enemy? Do you
want him to demonstrate compassionate love to others? Do
you want him to give his money and possessions to those
less fortunate? Do you want to see respect, responsibility,
and spiritual values springing up in him?

Then you must *teach* and *show* him. None of these qualities come accidentally. Not even church, Sunday school,
Bible camps, Christian school, or a vital youth group can do
the job that is left up to you alone. *You* are the one to teach
and lead. Your life will establish the direction for his life to
follow.

4. Instill Positive Self-esteem in Your Child

One of the key principles parents should instill in their child is positive self-esteem—the value he places on himself and his appraisal of how others view him. A man or woman with a healthy self-esteem regards himself highly, maintains a sense of confidence and peace, and is able to regard others highly as well. Low self-esteem fills one with a sense of inadequacy, worthlessness, and inferiority.

A child's concept of himself is influenced by several factors: who he *really* is, who he *thinks* he is, who *others* think he is, and who he *wishes* he could be. How he perceives himself and how others respond to him can ultimately be more significant than what he actually is. The greater the discrepancy between the real self and the perceived self, the greater the frustration he experiences. If he perceives himself as different from how he really is, while another person views him in another light, and he wishes he were something different still, he will experience great anxiety. But when he knows who he is, when that's who he wants to be, and when that's how people view him, he will have great peace and contentment.

When there is such a harmony of perception, a child is able to mature confidently. Your role is to help your children define their self-perceptions and harmonize the "I am, I think, they think, I wish" factors.

If a child has an improper regard for his own person-hood, everything else a parent attempts to teach is in vain. Children are soft and pliable, but like clay they steadily harden through the years. Their self-esteem must be established early.

Hindrances to Good Self-esteem

One of a child's basic drives is the desire to discover who he is. Minute-by-minute he gradually forms a self-concept. He entered the world knowing little about himself, but as he grows he eagerly tries to unearth what "makes him tick," what his value is, and what his capabilities are.

He grasps at every clue that will provide additional insight. He listens with his mind wide open to every word about himself and watches the responses of others. Everything is filed into his memory. Ultimately he will become the sum total of all he has heard about himself.

He is not "fishing" for compliments. A young child is a virgin field. He doesn't know what he is like, so he looks to adults and friends to tell him. A youngster thinks a grown-up is all-knowing and all-wise. He trusts and believes what adults say. He doesn't know whether their points of view are true or not. He merely digests the words and eventually forms his personality to conform to those words. He listens to what others think and adopts their perspectives as his own.

WHAT HE HEARS, HE BECOMES—it's as simple as that.

You as a parent are the most important person in this process, because your child values *your* opinions more highly than anyone else's. He will believe almost everything you say, true or not. Your words have enormous impact. Your responses to his behavior will shape his motivations, abilities, and self-confidence. Everything you communicate, however subtle, will greatly affect the molding of his slowly developing self-concept.

The shaping of a self-concept occurs imperceptibly. Few parents knowingly damage their child's self-esteem. Yet if he is habitually criticized, your child will grow to think poorly of himself. If he is told or thinks he is told such things as, "You are fat . . . lazy . . . clumsy . . . stupid," he will unconsciously live up to those judgments. Whether the statements were true or false will make no difference. He was born with a blank "tape" in his subconscious. Any input he receives will be recorded on that tape. The information in that recording is interpreted and he then decides what sort of person others perceive him to be.

Many parents confer negative characteristics upon their children while unaware of the dismal outcome they are prescribing for them. Most parents love their children and maintain lofty expectations for them. They want them to be attractive, contented, and successful, not fat, bungling, and slothful. Yet they steer their children's subconsciouses toward those negative traits by using the wrong words. The mind is amazing. It can turn people's words around and attach meanings to them never intended. Expressions of indifference, though unintentional, can scar a personality. Even what would normally be an acceptable comment, if said in exasperation, with a derogatory tone of voice, can cause such damage.

It isn't enough for you as a parent to avoid obvious condemnation. For a positive self-concept to develop, you must deliberately enter words on your child's blank "tape" that can be translated, "I am worth something." Stray comments do not "bounce off." Every word adds to the "programming" inside a child and dictates what he will one day become. He will become what he is told (however subtly) he is. As his conscoius mind receives words, emotions, experiences, and people's reactions to him, they are all registered in the subconscious mind, then processed into the personality. Only the grace of God can help to "erase" all that data and reverse its effects.

Negative words can slip out so easily, especially from a

What He Is Told, He Becomes

A child who hears, or thinks he hears, "You are a stupid child," will become a stupid child, though his IQ is 125. Another who receives the incoming message, "You are creative," will emerge as a creative youngster, though his IQ may be only 90.

father who tends to be jokingly sarcastic. Though you may consider your comments to be innocent or in lighthearted jest, your child may think otherwise. He reads beneath the surface. However harmless your intentions, negativism in any form is deadly, biting deep into your child. Your mannerisms, your tone of voice, the frustration you reveal with a glance or sigh all imply much about your inner feelings.

An innocent, "You can do better than that," to my son strikes painfully. If I say to a friend, "Gregory is going to be a great athlete—you ought to see him swing a bat!" but say nothing about Gregory's brother silently looking on, I may have communicated disapproval to him. My unpraised son would infer that I considered him unskilled, undeserving of my commendation, unable to meet my expectations and unable to compete with his brother. Actually my love for him may be tremendous, but I could still give him an inaccurate picture of how I perceived him. If I often said such things, he could suffer from my carelessness for the rest of his life, always thinking that he couldn't measure up to my standards.

The devastating results of parental criticism are all too common. We all know many like June in the following quote, though we may not realize it. Be honest and ask yourself, "Am I even now creating a future June in my own child?"

> June stared down at the floor. She was a bright, attractive, caring person, but she was obsessed with feelings of having been mistreated and short-changed in life. Her hurt ran deep:
>
> "It's the hell of being torn by the realization that nobody really loves me. I feel so rejected. I feel totally unacceptable and incompetent at everything I try to do. The more I try to change, the more I fail. . . .
>
> "Sometimes I feel like I'm intelligent and even creative inside. Those thoughts are pushed out when I remember what my parents kept telling me. I used to rebel because I

thought they were just sarcastic putdowns, but *perhaps my parents were right.* The more I fight, the more those memories haunt me.

"I hate myself because I blame my parents, and then feel so guilty. Sometimes I hate them so intensely, but they are my parents and I want them to love me so much. I want them to love me for who I am so badly I could scream. The longer I live the less I get done, and I don't feel worth anything unless I can get something done. At times I want to kill myself, but I can't because I'm afraid death will be too much like the hell I'm carrying around in my head now. My Christian friends tell me to let go and let God give me peace. They just don't know the pain. I'm so confused. I want to be loved physically, but sex seems so dirty. It's too painful anymore to be accepted by anyone. My friends keep telling me how I should feel if I am a Christian. Perhaps I'm not really a Christian at all. . . ."[6]

Children constantly compare themselves to their peers and to our expectations with very temporal yardsticks. The youngster who never receives compliments soon assumes that in adult eyes he is not as competent—and therefore as worthwhile—as his bigger, faster, stronger, prettier, smarter peers.

Children have several strikes against them from the very start of their search for self-esteem. During the first years of life they *are* inferior in many ways to most people they see regularly. They are smaller, less coordinated, less informed, less able to communicate, and are lower in authority, knowledge, and skills. Someone else is always telling them what to do and parents repeatedly drill in the message that most of what they attempt turns out wrong. And if a helpless baby brother or sister comes along, the younger one gets more attention! There is no way the child can win!

Though physical and mental skills develop as he grows older, they don't necessarily help. Wherever the unsuspecting youngster turns, he receives negative responses. The papers he brings home from school have red marks all over them. The only things marked are his errors. The only thing he has to gauge his progress by is the brilliant red 20% or 30%. He isn't told about, nor does he remember, the unmarked 70% or 80% that are *right*. Whatever he does we make sure he confronts his failures. At recess or at after-school games his teachers, coaches, and friends are quick to point out his weaknesses, his mistakes, or his clumsiness. But no one ever cheers his best efforts. No one seems to notice.

Even in church he often encounters such a negative reception. A popular tract designed to tell children the "good news" emphasizes that we are all black with sin. The average Christian mentality seems often to begin with the negative. We tell children the story of Moses (where the children are all killed) more often than we tell of Jesus' sitting children on His lap. It's no surprise that a young mind can draw negative conclusions about himself from that type of input.

Humans—children especially—thrive on positive feelings about themselves. You must communicate some *good* news to your child about himself! We are created to love and relate to other people, and the better our self-esteem the better our ability to do that. Providing a child a positive view of himself will enable him later to obey the most basic command for human relations—"You shall love your neighbor as yourself."

How to Instill Positive Self-esteem

Here is a magnificent challenge for you as a parent. If you implant positive words of kindness, respect, sensitivity, and love, your child will think of himself in a positive light. As he absorbs positive words, they will stimulate a self-concept of worth which leads to self-acceptance and confidence. Very few children are *really* lazy, clumsy, unskilled, or stupid, but many think they are. It's because we respond to their efforts nonchalantly and don't pay close attention. God has given your child amazing intelligence, coordination, and perseverance. He launches into new adventures with courage and performs daring feats before you daily! You simply have to pay attention to see them take place.

Self-esteem has two halves: feeling good about *who I am* and feeling good about *what I can do*. A person's self-respect is usually proportional to his ability to carry out tasks; he must possess certain capabilities. A person who feels good about his capabilities feels worthwhile and competent and can cope with life. Each small ability a child masters gives him enormous pride. As he grows and his proficiency in larger and greater tasks increases, his self-assurance increases as well.

It is far easier to maintain a negative stance toward your child's accomplishments than a positive stance. It is easy to greet your second grader's papier-mâché "house" with an indifferent grunt. But instead, lay down your newspaper, take the awkward creation in your hand, examine it carefully, lift your wide-eyed son into your lap and say, "This is really great! I like the shape and the color. Did you design it all by yourself? Could we put it on the mantle for a little while so that other people can see what a good job you did?"

That takes *effort*! But you will have communicated a number of thoughts to your son. He will see that you are interested in his life, that you have time for him, that what he does is important to you, that you consider him skilled, that you appreciate his creativity, and that he is more important to you than the newspaper. In just four or five minutes you will have made a substantial positive contribution to his sense of value.

Approval is fundamental to every person's well-being. We flourish or wither depending on the approval or disap-

receive. Parents often fail to see just how often ransmit either approval or disapproval; the careless us often have the most significant effect. And the results of such random input into a child's mind can be devastating. Many parents realize too late that they have been instilling negative self-concepts to their children which they may live with all their lives.

Negative response habits can be broken if parents determine to communicate approval and affirmation at every opportunity. Parents must base their responses to the child on God's value standards. God's values stand in marked contrast to society's preoccupation with appearance, athletic ability, fashion and popularity. But a Christian is not immune to such a value system. For example, recently my wife was observing a children's Sunday school class at our church. As class was about to begin, a little girl walked in—an ugly duckling sort—and was brusquely told, "Now go hang up your jacket. Come on now, hurry up, we're ready to start!" Several minutes later another girl walked in— cute, with a winning smile. She was a favorite of all the teachers and the daughter of one of the church's leading couples. The teacher's response was dramatically different. "Well hello, Mary, how nice you look today! Here, let me help you with your coat—we'll hang it up right over here. Say hello to Mary, everyone."

Both were well-behaved girls. But the response they received was vastly different. The false value system of the world had crept in.

Children are generally more confident about what their mothers think of them because positive feelings seem to flow more readily from women than men. Also, a father is usually with his children for less time so has less opportunity to communicate. The children often just don't know how Dad feels; he isn't as close to the daily, hour-by-hour family situation. So his innermost thoughts can remain a secret. Therefore when he is home they are intensely curious to know what he thinks and will look for any indication of his inner feelings. Unaware of their scrutiny, he may be short or have no time to speak much to the children. Therefore he may easily contribute to a negative self-identity in his children.

However, this very difficulty also gives a father tremendous advantage. Because his approval is generally more difficult to gain, it is all the more potent when received. An interested and encouraging father can make miraculous things happen in his child. His approval is deemed more important than anyone's.

The appreciated child is happy and well-adjusted; he feels respected, valued, and trusted, and can harmonize the various perceptions of himself.

A family atmosphere of affirmation and appreciation allows a child to develop his maximum potential. A parent should never cease searching for new ways to tell his child how much he loves and appreciates him. This will also help the child to see God the Father as a loving positive person, rather than as a demanding tyrant.

Don't be concerned that the painting was impossible to decipher, the football pass was wobbly, the cookies were hard as rocks, or that the mowing job wasn't quite perfect. You are shaping a personality, so what difference do a few imperfections make? Concern yourself with the magnificence of his efforts. Then you can truthfully exclaim, "This is wonderful!"—because at a child's level of maturity and skill, it probably is! You would expect better cookies from your wife or the bakery, but for your daughter's first attempt, they are the finest in the world.

If my eight-year-old son is learning to throw a football through a tire I've hung in the backyard, he needs encouragement. If his delivery isn't good, I compliment his stance. If that is bad, I applaud his perseverance. There's always something commendable. I take Don Highlander's advice that " . . . the hallmark of becoming a responsible parent is learning to be an encouraging parent." [7]

When your child is young, *avoid focusing on the results of his efforts.* It's easy to dish out a lukewarm commendation when results are up to adult standards, but a youngster needs cheers long before he is capable of great results.

As I teach my son to throw a pass, if I'm result-oriented, I will criticize every throw and continually correct the positioning of his elbow, feet, and fingers. Before long he will be discouraged, then lose interest, and quit.

But if I commend him on every pass, keep my corrections to a minimum and continue to encourage him after 49 misses in a row, he will be motivated to keep practicing. Eventually he will spiral the ball throught the tire. If at seventeen he is in line for a starting spot as quarterback, he'll need my experienced eye to reveal every flaw I can spot. But at eight, when his hand can barely grip the ball, much less rifle it thirty yards, he needs only my praise and admiration. My responsibility at the moment is to build his inner qualities, which will eventually be reflected outwardly in practiced skills.

Teach Your Child Skills

Anything which gives a child a good feeling about himself raises his or her self-esteem. Possessing a wide range of physical skills increases this sense of confidence and proficiency. Though you must always emphasize that our significance lies in who we *are* in God, a child's sense of self-value is very dependent on his ability to *do* things well.

This aspect of your child's needs can be provided by teaching and exposing him to a variety of skill-producing activities. A toddler needs puzzles, blocks, and jungle-gyms. A preschooler needs trips to the park and playground; he needs to romp in the woods, climb trees, throw rocks, swing on ropes, and run on the beach. He needs toys that spark his mechanical interests and abilities. Then as he grows he can learn to cook, sew, sing, play an instrument, and hit, catch, kick, throw, and dribble balls. He doesn't have to be the best, but he should acquire these various skills. But, if these skills are neglected and a child's performance in noticeably inferior—always the slowest, the first to get caught, the last one chosen—his peers will deride him and his self-esteem will disintegrate.

Make no strict delineation between masculine and feminine activities. The more things your child can do, the more self-confidence he will have. A girl should be able to play in sports just as a boy should be able to iron shirts and cook meals. Every child should learn basic musical skills and should especially be exposed to playing the piano. Later you can introduce him to handtools—hammers, saws, levels, clamps, tape measures, etc., so he can learn to make things. In *The Mother's Almanac* we read:

> The more your child is allowed to expand, in every direction, the better he can express himself. These expressions take many forms. While one child might speak best with words, another uses his easel or his carpenter's kit, and still another prefers clay or needle and thread or a suitcase full of dress-ups. This doesn't mean he'll automatically be an actor, a writer, or a builder when he grows up, but his preferences often point out his talents. Unless he has the chance to sample a little bit of everything, he may never find out where these talents lie.[8]

Obviously you will emphasize different skills than I would, but the more well-rounded your child's exposure the better he will be able to participate on a par with his friends. He will develop confidence in his own abilities, he will be eager to launch into new ventures, and he will walk with his head held high.

Share a Child's World

It is easy to be preoccupied with your own affairs and convey little enthusiasm for those things your child is excited about. How sensitive are you to his world? Do you realize how much effort has gone into your three-year-old's scribbling which he has proudly presented to you as you walked in the door after work? Do you realize how crushed he was when the next morning he watched you throw that same drawing into the trash with some of yesterday's junk mail? He poured his whole being into those few crayon marks and your interest was casual at best.

And what does your five-year-old think after spending a half hour cleaning his room and arranging his toys, hoping to impress you, if you walk in and say, "This room's a mess. Why don't you put your toys away?"

Certainly by adult standards children do not possess great wisdom, remarkable ideas, or amazing talent. But you must do as God does. He is able to *see potential*. He looks at the raw material and sees how great a youngster's accomplishments really are.

But we are so busy. We thoughtlessly put them off. How often do you carelessly fling about phrases such as, "Wait a minute . . . not now, I'm busy . . . I'll look at it later . . . I've got my hands full . . . We'll go there another day . . . don't bother me now . . . "? If your child receives such responses often, he will conclude that Mom and Dad's affairs take priority over his own. He may then say to himself, "I am not as important to my parents as other things," and thus develop a sense of low personal worth.

Jesus, who is our example, approached children very differently. Whenever young ones approached Him, Jesus took time from His busy schedule (full of important things to do, important people to talk with, important things to say) to be with them. He was sensitive to their world.

When your child first begins to reach cautiously out of himself to do something he has never tried before, that is a crucial moment in his life. Respond with praise, no matter what the result may be—a silly poem, an unrecognizable wood-working project, a screeching clarinet solo, or a clumsy free-throw attempt. The very act of trying, of launching into new regions of accomplishment, is worthy of high praise.

Don't masquerade your criticism as a back-door compliment by saying, "You can do better than that!" Your child who has just poured his all into the effort is not interested in how well you think he might do ten years from now. You will never spur him on to greater heights with such negative rejoinders. *He needs to know that he has succeeded—today!* Tell him you are proud of him!

When a bright-eyed youngster is gunned down with a you-can-do-better evaluation, he senses only one thing—today I failed. What a blow to the motivation to accomplish more of the same, to keep practicing. It is no wonder that by the time many children reach junior high they have little desire for schoolwork, athletics, or accomplishments of any kind. Too many of their ventures which showed faint glimmers of latent abilities were smothered with wet blankets of criticism. Motivation has been undercut one small comment at a time.

The Line of Acceptable Behavior

All parents unconsciously draw a line of acceptable behavior to mark the difference between what they consider acceptable and unacceptable actions and attitudes. To a large degree a child's self-esteem is formed not on the basis of his actions, but on the basis of our responses. If you draw the line of acceptable behavior unrealistically high and thus frequently give a negative response, your child will realize that most of his actions fall below your line and are therefore unacceptable.

However, if you take a more relaxed stance and draw the line at a realistic level without compromising your disciplinary standards, then your child will be apt to feel accepted and worthwhile because the majority of his actions falls above the line and is positively received.

In either case your child's actions can be identical. The only variable is the position of the line. If the line is lower, most of what your child does is acceptable to you. If the line is high, most of his efforts will be rejected. Your child will

Unrealistically high line of acceptable behavior

Most of a child's actions fall below the line and are therefore unacceptable to the parent.

The child views himself as a failure.

grow to feel accepted and valuable or rejected and worth-less, *simply on the basis of where you draw the line.* Two identical children can develop contrasting self-images if their parents respond differently to similiar actions and at-titudes.

A child may be skilled, polite, and intelligent, but if his parents continually demand perfection from him (drawing the line of acceptable behavior so high that 80% or 90% of what he does isn't quite good enough for them, he will even-tually think that he can never quite succeed no matter what he does. Even if his parents are unconscious of the condem-

Most of a child's actions falls above the line and is therefore acceptable to the parent.

The child views himself as successful. He feels accepted as he is.

A realistically placed line of acceptable behavior allows a child to be a child and does not place impossible expectations on him

nation they are doling out, the results will be the same. If the child *thinks* his behavior is not accepted, he will react with guilt and a sense of failure.

A Child Must Be a Child

Children need to express their feelings daily; they have to tell what's on their minds. In young children, because of their intellectual immaturity, much of their emotional expression is accomplished with their hands and feet. They run, play, draw, build, chase, climb, dress up and explore—all to express themselves. They don't care whether they have talent or whether their work is beautiful or skilled. They just want to "uncork" all that's pent up inside them. For them, that is expression and creation.

That's why hobbies, sports, music, books, puzzles, art materials, sandboxes, toys, and dirt piles are so vital for their growth. They provide youngsters with avenues for varied expressions. In such environments their abilities and good feelings about themselves soar—*if* their activities are greeted with enthusiasm and acceptance.

Without some failures people would never learn to cope with life. But successes should outweigh failures. *You* provide the sense of success for your child through encouraging responses. One child may play tennis, another the organ or guitar, another may collect lizards. But whatever their interests and abilities, they must each succeed.

Your child places higher value on your opinions than upon anyone else's. Therefore, if you say, "Great!" and he knows you mean it, all his peers can say, "Boo!" and it will hardly daunt his pride. He must know that *in your eyes* he is absolutely the best in the world. Even grossly low performance levels, which outside observers would deem failures, can be treated by you as gigantic accomplishments, thus boosting confidence and self-esteem. No matter how minor the visible progress, your enthusiastic praise will motivate your child to continue to learn. Motivation is set in motion by praise and fueled by further encouragement.

I have no intention of deceiving my children. I simply recognize the levels at which their efforts are being made. I don't compare them with achievements only attainable at a later age. Nearly *all* parents are guilty of expecting their children to be adults before their time—demanding from them too much too soon. *A child must be allowed to be a child.* Life for him is virgin territory and he has much to learn. Praise and support early in life provide a good perspective of himself and will result in good performances and good attitudes later.

At every age of his development, your child wants to involve you in his life. You must take the time to do this. From his point of view nothing could be more exciting than to show you his fort, to have you throw him passes, to have you help him learn to ride his bike or to help fix the evening meal.

Young boys especially need opportunities to prove themselves physically; it affects them deeply when their parent is there to watch and encourage them. Their parent is saying, "I'm available, I'm interested. You may always approach me without fear of being shut off. You are the most special person in the world to me. I enjoy watching you. Your opinions are valuable to me. I want to know everything you are learning."

Compare such a response to the icy, "What's that?" response to a child's prized drawing. Imagine how a child envisions God the Father if all he ever gets from his parents is scorn.

But your child does not remain immature forever. Though you must allow him to be a child when young, as he grows in wisdom and ability, you must gradually hand "the reins" of his life to him. Increasing freedom and independence must be met with corresponding responsibility. And the more latitude you give him and the more capably he performs under such liberty, the stronger and more mature he will feel. If you continually provide experiences for him to "try his wings," he will discover the success of being able to stand on his feet. You must be sensitive to the maturity of each child, for each progresses at a different rate. The process inches forward by degrees. Don't hasten it but allow it to happen at its own pace.

A maturing child, when secure in the leadership of his parents, moves out a little further all the time, takes increasingly greater risks and experiences the satisfaction of self-development. He will begin to work out some of his own problems and to use more of his own judgment and insight. Such success in later years will depend on the quality of his early training. If he knows you trust and respect him, he will not only have confidence in himself, but will feel free to come to you for counsel and support. As he prepares to face the world, a teen-ager needs to know his parents are right there whenever they are needed. A teenager is a questioning and groping young adult; when he encounters rough waters, the support of a loving parent reinforces his foundations of self-esteem and confidence.

5. Discipline and Training—What's the Difference?

Two ingredients give a child's life a strong foundation—*discipline* and *training*. They are separate only in the way that gravel and cement are separate ingredients of the concrete which undergirds a building. Once the concrete is mixed, poured, and cured the two become one. Similarly, training techniques and disciplinary methods, though separate, often can hardly be distinguished from each other.

Yet even though gravel and cement become inseparable, they do perform different functions in the concrete. Discipline and training also, though inseparable, address different needs in your child's nature and you need to understand this distinction in order to effectively meet both needs.

A relationship with God requires obedience. Therefore you must teach your child to respect and obey parental authority so that he will also live in submission to God's authority. *Discipline is primarily intended to instill obedience.*

You must also train your child to live a respectful, responsible and independent life in society. You must teach him desirable habits so that he can regulate and control himself. *Training is designed to teach social behavior, skills, and responsibility.*

65

Obedience arises from the attitude of the heart, but behavior is formed by habit.

Training and Discipline:
Positive and Negative Guidance

Jesus' parable of the wise and foolish builders teaches us that building a firm foundation requires digging down below the sand and loose soil to solid bedrock. That is where you build the foundations for your child's life—on the solid rock of God's Word.

The Bible teaches that God *disciplines* those He loves, that discipline is integral with love, that a parent who does not discipline his child does not love him, and that there is no better way to raise a godless child than to withhold discipline from him (Prov. 3:12; 13:24; 29:15; Heb. 12:6; Rev. 3:19).

Training is necessary for success in all areas of life. Nothing left to itself will mature to full potential. A garden without care will become choked with weeds. An orchard without pruning will become a grove of barren trees. A student without a teacher will aimlessly grope for truth. An athlete is trained by a coach, a horse by a trainer and jockey, and a musician by a maestro.

A child is no different. If left to himself, a person will sink into depravity. The Scriptures describe the human heart as "deceitful above all things, and desperately corrupt . . . " (Jer. 17:9). Of all of God's created beings, man has the greatest capacity for good or evil. Therefore a child stands in the greatest need of training and discipline for his godly potential to be realized.

And God has established the family as the institution to supply a child with the necessary discipline and training. He has sovereignly chosen parents to accept leadership and to maintain order in family relationships. In this capacity, the father and mother are to bring their child (as well as themselves) to his highest reaches of maturity.

When a child is very young it seems all his training is correctional—a parent must say "no" to everything. But soon teaching is blended in. By the time he is twelve the process has nearly reversed—you are correcting very little and teaching a great deal.

Discipline and training, therefore, are the two facets of the strategy you must use to navigate your child into the mainstream of life. Both have certain negative and positive qualities; but the end results are entirely beneficial for his growth.

The Interrelationship of Training and Discipline

These two aspects of parenting mix and flow in such a way that in practical daily living it is often nearly impossible to distinguish them. We will now dissect the two—discipline and training—for much the same reason a boy takes a clock apart: to see how it works and to understand it more thoroughly. But the boy knows the clock cannot work when its pieces are scattered all over the table. When he puts it back together, the gears and ratchets function as a unit—together. The individual components are no longer even visible.

It is the same with discipline and training. Life with children is complex. There will be times when both rebellion and childish actions (attitudes *and* behavior) are bound together in a situation. You will then have to draw upon all the understanding you possess to arrive at a solution. You may have to spank, isolate, and employ natural consequences for just the one incident. But it is important that you apply each particular method to the particular need for which it was designed. You spank to curb rebellion and employ natural consequences to change behavior. But if you spank primarily to change behavior or try to talk your child out of his disobedience, your efforts will prove fruitless. It's difficult to differentiate, during the heat of the moment, which type of behavior the child has committed. You must, therefore, develop a good understanding of the methods and of your child.

The need for training a child to function in society is widely recognized. But many parents and modern child psychologists are oblivious to a child's need to learn respect and obedience. Secular psychology operates on a basis which largely denies, even scoffs at, the biblical need to submit to God and others. Parents who entertain these concepts find their focus blurred. They have heard "outmoded" disciplinary techniques condemned as harsh, ineffective, and useful only in desperate circumstances. Such unsuspecting parents try in vain to "teach" their children good attitudes, but attitudes can be dealt with only through discipline, not training.

Using training methods to deal with rebellion is like trying to talk a lion out of pouncing on you—your arguments may be very convincing, but he understands a different kind of "argument." Words can do little to change an insurgent heart.

There is an opposite problem among many Christians who have raised the banner of discipline. They have failed to see that *discipline* is not a tool intended primarily to alter *behavior* patterns at all. Thus, they resort to discipline in dealing with any undesirable behavior, regardless of the motive. This type of disciplinary policy makes no consideration for a child's physical or mental immaturity which may have contributed to the behavior.

Focusing on either area, and excluding the other, will probably cause a child to be confused about right and wrong. A proper focus must include a thorough recognition of both needs—discipline and training—in a child.

6. Discipline: Molding Attitudes and Shaping the Will

The Right to Lead

We have all been duped by the modernistic trends of humanism, and now authority in our culture is losing ground. No longer do men sense their responsibility to strongly lead their wives. No longer do parents consider it their right or obligation to assertively lead their children. "Equality" has become a misnomer for a leaderless society in which authority is challenged on every front. Husbands have abdicated their roles. Parents have abdicated their roles. Even employers no longer tell their employees what to do; instead there is discussion, negotiation, and "co-management" where everyone is addressed on the same level.

The humanists to whom the world ignorantly bows insist that children need to be free from adult leadership, even parental authority. The campaign for children's rights has gone to such absurd lengths as to advocate that children have financial, sexual, and vocational equality with adults. Spanking is illegal in some parts of the world, and such a law is drawing closer to reality in the United States as well.

We Christians have naively been swept along by this un-

69

godly wave of change. We have silently bowed out, abandoning the roles God assigned to us. God never intended for men to be harsh taskmasters over their wives or for parents to crack the whip over the heads of their children. But He *did* intend that parents lead their children strongly and assertively in all aspects of family life. Parents are to protect their children, seek God's guidance on their behalf, battle for them against the negative forces that would erode their self-esteem, and build up their faith in God, raising them to their full stature in Christ. *This* is to be our role as fathers and mothers—a forceful and dynamic role, full of God's authority to take command with loving humility and self-sacrifice and guide our children into the full potential God intended for them.

Even to Christians parenthood is no longer the exalted and purposeful role it once was. Parent and child now grow up side by side rather than the parent *leading* his child into adulthood. Today's men and women are uncomfortable with talk of being in charge. They are reticent to boldly assert themselves, make decisions and stand up for the authority that is theirs in God.

But children need adult authority. Parents were created to lead, to initiate, and to direct. When children are permitted to govern themselves and roam freely during their younger years, they are the most frustrated creatures imaginable. Larry Christenson notes:

> An infant knows whether or not he can manipulate his parents, and if he can, he will. . . . Don't be afraid to be boss. Children need to know there is someone stronger and wiser in the family.[9]

As a parent you must lay aside timidity and begin to provide loving, strong headship over your child. You are *not*, as the world would tell you, on an equal level with your child. You *do* possess the right to direct and guide his life. It is *you* who is called to mold him and to shape his will, attitudes, and values. This is your right, your responsibility, and your challenge. Such a firm stance is the basis from which to discipline.

All discipline must be approached within the context of what you are trying to accomplish in your child's life. Discipline is only one component of the parenting process; it provides no solution to anything in itself but is a base upon which to build. Therefore, parents who discipline for discipline's sake accomplish little. But purposeful discipline will help your child reach his potential, teach him his proper place in God's order, and shape his will so that he can eventually offer himself for service to his Maker.

Understanding Correction

Children must be *taught* to obey. This is not a negative issue, but a very practical one. All humans, as Isaiah writes, turn "every one to his own way" (Isa. 53:6). Sticking to the rules is something we prefer not do. We seek for every loophole, every excuse, to justify disobedience.

Therefore you must introduce your child to one of life's most basic principles: there are certain standards he *must* conform to; there are certain rules to follow—certain things are right, certain things are wrong—and there are temporal and eternal consequences which result from disregarding them.

Discipline is above all *preparatory*. It teaches a child to function in a world that has a certain order and requires, in a particular sense, a degree of conformity. A society stands or falls on the basis of individual obedience to God's precepts. There is no other way to live in harmony with God—or man. The ability to obey God in later life originates in a child's *learned* ability to obey his parents in early life.

Obedience is at the core of discipline. In a child's earliest years *correctional punishment* is the key to effective discipline. But punishment can be of two kinds: *judicial* and *redemptive*. Judicial punishment is a judgment or response to some action—a sentence against wrong-doing. Many parents discipline simply to punish for the wrong behavior. There is an action followed by a punishment. That's the end of it.

Redemptive punishment, on the other hand, is foresightful. The punishment is not simply a quick response nor an end in itself. If a parent is always thinking ahead, the punishment he gives is designed as a lesson which will be valuable later on. It is corrective, positive and redemptive.

God's love for His people is clearly seen in His frequent use of redemptive discipline. Though in the moment of pain, discipline may seem unbearable, the motive behind it is one of love and tenderness. God wants to purify His people and bring them to maturity. To achieve this He must discipline us—not as a judgment against us but to teach us the ways that will ultimately bring the greatest joy and fulfillment.

This is the discipline which provides children with a strong foundation of obedience. Their punishments are meant to teach valuable lessons (e.g., spanking a child for getting too near a fire or wandering out in the street). Such discipline is a carefully planned, loving response which offers a useful and important lesson of life.

God's ways, like those of a wise parent, are always purposeful. So must be the discipline of our children. Quick, thoughtless, hasty responses accomplish little. Lashing out angrily in the heat of the moment has no place in effective parenting. Discipline must be carried out by a parent who is in full control.

The Discipline of Boundaries

In one sense, all discipline involves the boundaries you

establish for your child. They are the essence of a positive program of early training. A child needs them to feel comfortable and secure, to know how far he can go in a given situation.

God created the world with boundaries. They exist for our safety and our good. But before you can teach your child about God's boundaries which concern the greater issues of life, he must become accustomed to the limitations in the smaller scale of his own world. You must therefore teach your child to obey and live within the structure of the family in a manner parallel to that by which all men must live within the structure of God's order for the world.

As a parent it is your job to establish boundaries for your child and then do two things. First, offer affirmation and praise when he remains within those boundaries. And secondly, strictly enforce the boundaries you have set. When challenged you must promptly administer discipline.

This twofold approach (providing rewards and security within the limits, and giving discipline when the limits are challenged) builds respect, confidence, and obedience into a child. This approach, if consistently applied, reveals the character of God, for God definitely employs clear boundaries in His dealings with us. The principle of obeying (or disobeying) established standards, and boundaries pervades all of Scripture.

Each family will establish its own set of boundaries. There will be certain universal qualities, but the details will vary from family to family. To be effective, boundaries must be specific, set in advance, and clearly explained to your child. You must train yourself to convey exactly what you expect ("Don't touch that plant in the corner," NOT "Be a good girl."). The younger the child the more precise your language must be.

Be thoughtful and prayerful as you determine boundaries; don't merely make demands on your child for your own convenience. Always keep in mind the long-range benefits in the life of your child.

The most important universal boundary that must be enforced is open rebellion. When a child willfully defies his parent's authority, he must be disciplined immediately. Cold, calculating disobedience (slamming his truck against the wall, while looking you right in the eye, immediately after you have calmly told him to place it back in the toy box) can be met only one way by a parent who hopes to keep his authority intact—with a swift, calmly administered spanking. Respect for and obedience to authority are standards you must consistently enforce or else undermine your child's future relationship with God. Respect and obedience to God, hinge on learning respect and obedience to parents.

Do not set so many limits that you are unable to enforce them consistently. It is better to exercise tight control over a half-dozen than to be indecisive about thirty. The only thing worse than having no limits is to have rules and ignore them. Draw the lines wide enough so your child has plenty of space to run and play freely without fear of accidentally crossing some line he has forgotten about. The boundaries will not accomplish their purpose if they overly inhibit a child. But the boundaries which limit what is allowed must be solidly enforced.

It's often hard for a Christian parent, trying to be loving and sensitive, to spank a child for something that seems small. But by "letting it go this time," he gradually allows himself to become inconsistent, sympathetic, and dominated—by his child. By refusing to insist upon obedience, a parent does his child a permanent disservice, though at the moment it seems easier to back down than to carry through. If a parent allows his child to determine his own behavior, the child will conclude that he is his own master and grow up having no concept of proper authority.

The relationship of a parent with his child is a model of

the parent's relationship with God. Certainly God does not allow us full control over our own lives. He doesn't give us everything we desire, nor does He allow us to go our own way unhindered. He knows the devastating consequences.

Similiarly, we do our children permanent harm by catering to their every whim and fancy. Just as God sets boundaries for our lives, which have predictable consequences if ignored, we must set them for our children as well.

God made us so that ultimate joy and satisfaction can be attained only if we live according to His laws. When we disobey God, we immediately hinder the blessings He has for us. It's the same for a child. God made him to thrive in the love and security of a family. A child is most content when he knows exactly what the boundaries are. He *wants* the lines securely drawn. He doesn't want to be left on his own.

The Need to Discipline

When the boundaries are challenged, the child's disobedience must be firmly met with loving and consistent discipline.

When the Boundaries Are Challenged

Your boundaries *will* be tested for two primary reasons. First, your child may simply try to determine if a stated limit still exists. So he gives it a nudge, just to see what you will do. If you respond as always, then he knows the boundary is still to be reckoned with.

Second, he may test a boundary because he feels insecure. If he is unsure of what exactly is expected of him, he will push out toward the boundary trying to determine at what point it becomes inflexible. He wants to know precisely how far he can go. When a parent consistently stands firm on a certain issue, the child knows exactly what to expect. But if the parent waffles on every decision, the child can become insecure. He will try desperately to discover where his parents will stand firm.

If "yes" means maybe, and "no" usually means nothing, a child will disobey. He will continue to disobey until he finds exactly where his parents will take action. This is not because of what some consider "inborn" rebellion, but simply because of insecurity arising out of unclear standards. A child needs solid handles to hang onto. His seemingly unruly behavior may be nothing but an attempt to make his parents define their words through *action*. When a parent says "no" and the child disobeys and nothing happens, he has learned something about his mother or father's definition of the word "no." So he will try it again if necessary. He is merely seeking a definition. (Such disobedience should not be confused with defiance, an altogether different case.)

Finally the parent exclaims in an angry outburst, "I can't understand that boy! He never does a thing I say!" This parent is confused about what is actually going on. The silent plea of the child is going unheeded. Through dis-

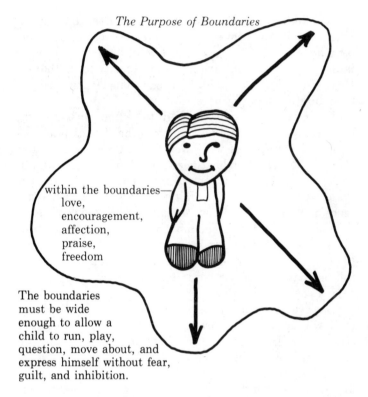

The Purpose of Boundaries

within the boundaries—
love,
encouragement,
affection,
praise,
freedom

The boundaries
must be wide
enough to allow a
child to run, play,
question, move about, and
express himself without fear,
guilt, and inhibition.

obedience he may be trying to say, "I want to know where my limits are. I'm insecure when I don't know."

When a child does cross a line, and is disciplined, there seems to be a subconscious satisfaction in knowing that he has found the boundary. He is secure in the knowledge that it has held firm. A child consistently disciplined for disobedience of clearly defined standards has found an authority he knows he can trust. He knows his parents are strong. He knows the meaning of their words. He knows they won't waver, for they have stood the test. He senses freedom and love.

A child whose parents exercise well-planned and reasonable discipline is contented. No four-year-old or six-year-old *wants* to be in charge, despite what his actions seem to indicate. God did not give him the capacity for authority. He created him to live under loving, strong leaders who will raise him up knowing how to obey.

It is a myth that children want to be free. On their own, children quickly seek order and routine. Chaos unnerves them. They are secure when well-defined limits exist about them. School children have been observed to be more inhibited when no fence surrounds their playing area than if there were a fence. Our children instantly began playing more freely the moment we installed a low redwood fence around our front lawn. Though it's an easy matter to crawl under it or hop over it, and though it offeres no visible protection, it brought a marked freedom to run, tumble and roll on that part of our yard. The boundary of that fence gave a sense of security.

But even a secure child whose boundaries are rigid and clear will occasionally disobey just to make sure they are still there. The most angelic of children seem to need to check the boundaries periodically and make sure that all is as it should be—that the boundaries are still being enforced. If the boundaries remain intact and disobedience is forcefully dealt with, the child will mature as an obedient and contented child. He is assured that Mom and Dad are in charge. Later he will find submission to God all the more natural because he has learned to live under the loving and consistent authority of his parents.

The Results of Vague Boundaries

Unpredictable boundaries do not allow for consistent training. A child growing in such an atmosphere will become increasingly disobedient as he desperately attempts to locate a solid, inflexible line he can trust as a limit to his actions. Finding none he continues to push further and further, becoming more unmanageable all the time.

A child who is forced to live in such instability gradually loses respect for his parents. Disobedience that stems from an honest desire to know where the boundaries are only gets worse. The selfish will grows stronger and soon becomes a major problem. After a few years the desire to submit to the authority behind recognizable boundaries is all but gone. Now he wants to be in control and woe to anyone who stands in his way!

Spineless parents initiate two problems in their children. One, they grow up not knowing how to obey. Two, they lose respect for authority as their own self-will is allowed to dominate. Their disobedience, which began from a simple need to find and live by firm limits, eventually hardens into total self-centeredness. Ultimately a teen-ager (who becomes an adult) submits to no one and cares for no one but himself. The child who has thus controlled his parents loses all respect for them, for he knows better than anyone that their leadership is as firm as warm milk. They did not stand up to him. Even when he was small he easily manipulated them.

Such disrespect will be demonstrated more and more openly. Not only will he reject his parents' authority, he will reject all they stand for. And since his response to all authority is solidified in his relationship with his parents, he learns to disparage other authority as well. It's no wonder he cannot form an adequate concept of God; his background holds no consistent, firm authority-figure.

What contrast to the child who grows up under strong authority. The boundaries, clearly established through the years, imply, "When you are told to do something, you do it." By forming such limits, his parents have indirectly said, "We will not make unreasonable or embarrassing demands on you. We love and respect you. Everything we do for you or to you is meant for your ultimate good."

A consistent parent earns the trust and respect of his child through considerate and loving use of his authority. His basic position, however, never changes—"When I tell you something, you heed my words. If you choose to disobey, you will be disciplined. I will enforce what I say. I love you too much to allow you to disobey without being punished. I must teach you to obey so that you will be able to relate to the world and to God. So believe me, if you choose to disobey me, you will regret it. My love compels me to back up my words."

From the child's perspective, especially in his early years, it does not even matter whether his parents are necessarily right every time. They won't be. But they are to be obeyed regardless. The Bible says bluntly, "Children, obey your parents" (Eph. 6:1).

But this gives parents no license to abuse their God-given authority. Paul also warns, "Fathers, do not provoke your children to anger, but bring them up in the discipline and instruction of the Lord" (Eph. 6:4).

As a child grows, his relationship with authority changes. His parents will discuss issues with him and allow him a greater role in the training process. His freedom and responsibility within the family grows with maturity.

This parallels our relationship with God. He must teach us to obey willingly without questioning his authority. Then after we have proved obedient in small matters, He is able to lead us into greater responsibility and freedom. He allows us wider latitude in making decisions and places increasingly greater decisions in our hands.

So must it be in the raising of your child. The foundation of complete submission must first be laid—the will must be shaped. Then he can grow and mature and be given authority. But unless his will is brought into subjection *first*, he cannot mature properly because he will only know how to go his own way.

The Spanking

The spanking is the classic disciplinary tool. Numerous scripture passages confirm that God intended it to be used when we discipline our children (Prov. 20:30; 22:15; 23:13-14; Heb.12:6-7). Pain is a marvelous teacher, one of the "voices" a youngster understands best.

When a parent first begins spanking (as soon as the child obviously understands "no"), it seems a harsh measure for such trifling disobedience. But unless one begins at that point, there will be no way to avoid the major clashes later on. Adolescence will be a composite of twelve to fifteen years of prior training. Anything not yet dealt with will surface then. A parent who loses the early confrontations with his child or pretends not to notice when a challenge is issued will find later conflicts harder to win and more difficult to resolve.

Therefore, you must overcome the hesitation, grit your teeth, realize the truth of, "This hurts me more than it does you," and spank your dear, tender, harmless little toddler. Know that the price you pay in personal agony during the early years will be repaid many times over as he matures to adulthood.

A spanking is quick and decisive. It is finished in seconds. Though the pain, crying, and emotional "bite" may linger for a few minutes, the need for hurt feelings, pouting and pent-up anger and bitterness is gone. Once administered, it is over. Like a cut, it heals. It does not grow and fester beneath the surface but clears the air like a rainstorm. Such punishment is just, momentary, and memorable.

The spanking is a tool and as such can be misused. Parents must perceive the enormity of their responsibility. Spanking should primarily be reserved for those moments of defiance, when a child challenges the boundary by consciously stepping across it. In such a situation he knows full well he is going counter to your instructions. There is no need for you to rage with anger or to punish impulsively. He has defied your authority and challenged the established limit; therefore you respond in complete control with well-measured swats. You must be just in your spanking, never arbitrary. And though painful, your love should somehow be expressed through a spanking. Your child should always be told why you spank and that as God's child you are compelled to teach your child obedience and to spank him when he disobeys.

The corrective discipline of spanking must be implemented to redirect wrong actions and attitudes. If incorrectly used, spanking will tear down and crush the spirit. Your job as a sensitive parent is to preserve and build up his spirit while working to break and bring under control his self-will. Only then will your son's or daughter's energies be channeled to serve God in later years.

Children won't "grow out" of rebellion. It must be *purged* from them. If they are not disciplined properly in the early years, their selfishness will grow and take on more subtle forms, gradually undermining the whole family structure.

Learn to tailor spankings to fit your child's unique temperament and his particular form of rebellion. Every situation will be slightly different. No pat formulas for *how* to spank will achieve the desired effect—to break the self-will and build up the spirit.

A strong-willed child may need a severe spanking, another child may come to full repentance with a mild one or a simple reprimand. Great sensitivity is necessary. Discipline is not intended to humiliate but to rein in the destructive will. It should, therefore, be administered privately, should have a definite beginning and end, and should then result in forgiveness and a restored relationship.

Ten Steps Toward Effective Discipline

Just as there are specific disciplinary tools, there are specific procedures to follow which insure that your discipline achieves its intended results. Bill Gothard makes the following suggestions:[10] (Adaptation of his material.)

See That a Child Accepts Responsibility for Disobedience

If a child is to repent, his offense must be clear in his mind. Discipline won't accomplish anything if he thinks he has done no wrong. Therefore, help clarify the problem by asking, "What did you do?" or by discussing the situation. If you accuse, he is apt to deny or justify what he did, or blame others. A simple confession is all you're after.

Discipline in Private

If you spank a youngster in the presence of others, he will be so conscious of what they are thinking that he will be unable to focus on his need to repent. This will make him look for ways to justify himself in their eyes. Therefore the discipline will prove ineffective.

Humiliating him in such a manner also erects a barrier for future communication between you and him. If you have embarrassed him in front of others, he will feel that you have betrayed your trust in him.

Silently Reflect on What Has Happened

A brief period of silence before the punishment gives the

child the opportunity to think about his offense. Hopefully he will see why the discipline is necessary. This may not always happen, but the silence provides the opportunity if it is to come. It also allows the parent's anger to be soothed as he quietly prays for wisdom and love.

Always Associate Love with Discipline

In God's design love and discipline spring from the same source. From his earliest spankings a child should be told that God instructs parents to discipline in order to instill obedience. We must also obey God and even receive His discipline (though different) in our own lives. Hebrews 12:5-7 should be our basis for discipline: "My son, do not regard lightly the discipline of the Lord, nor lose courage when you are punished by him. For the Lord disciplines him whom he loves, and chastises every son whom he receives! It is for discipline that you have to endure. God is treating you as sons; for what son is there whom his father does not discipline?"

Establish God as the Final Authority

If your son or daughter mistakenly believes that authority originates with *you*, he will feel much safer when he deceives and disobeys you than he would if he understood that God stands behind you. He must realize that you are in a chain of command which begins with God. He needs to see that whether you or he sins, God expects repentance in either case.

Spank with a Neutral Object

When spanking use something neutral (which the Bible calls a rod) rather than your hand. (I've found that a wooden spoon works well.) If you repeatedly spank with your hand, your child may begin to associate your hand with punishment. This would cause obvious problems when you try to use the same hand to hold him and express love. The use of a rod also further confirms your explanation that the need for discipline comes from beyond either parent or child and is based on God's laws rather than on your arbitrary judgments.

Discipline to the Proper Limit

Balance is critical. Too much spanking and too little spanking both have destructive effects. You must be sensitive to your child's will and spirit. You need to spank until the self-will breaks, then stop. Over-discipline will damage the spirit. You want to give sufficient discipline but as little as possible to achieve repentance.

Afterward Give Reassurance and Comfort

Once a spanking is over you need to shower assurances of love on your child so that he undertands that discipline and love are one. This is the time for hugs, tender words, wiped-away tears, and finally, smiles. This is a time when a young child is highly vulnerable. Sending him to his room after a spanking is a double punishment with no possibility of reconciliation. Once the discipline is over, it should be buried in the past. Ideally an after-spanking time of togetherness can lead to some shared activity. A fun time together afterward can joyfully restore the relationship.

Discuss Further Action That May Be Required

Correction for misbehavior sometimes involves not only repentance through a parent's discipline but also an acceptance of responsibility for the behavior. When others have been hurt or property has been damaged, some sort of restitution or apology is necessary. The child must face the consequences of what he has done and make the situation right.

Evaluate Yourself Humbly

As a parent you inevitably will make mistakes. You will not always discipline perfectly or fairly. You will encounter times when you have accused your child falsely or have spanked in anger. When you realize you have disciplined wrongly, you should go to your son or daughter and ask for forgiveness, preferably after some time has passed and emotions are calm.

Children have an acute sense of fair play. When a parent is too proud to apologize for mistakes, his relationship with the child is stunted. But when a child knows his parents try to be fair and have the courage to admit their blunders, he will submit to their discipline, knowing he will never be intentionally wronged.

The Many Dimensions of Discipline

The consistency with which we implement boundaries and spankings determine the value of early childhood training. Children are delicate. The spirit of a child can be easily bruised and his fragile self-esteem crushed if disciplinary techniques are misused. Discipline must be applied within the context of instilling self-esteem and teaching. Sloppy discipline can cause a distorted concept of self-worth.

Discipline changes as a child matures. Once the foundation is stable, boundaries can be gradually relaxed. This does not mean that an indecisive father forces everyone to live in constant uncertainty under rules thrown together as he meets problems. It simply means that as a child proves himself obedient, his parents may loosen his "reins" and trust him in wider areas of life. After all, he is being prepared for independence.

A maturing child grows increasingly aware of his parents' consistency and of the justice of their discipline. A child of three must obey regardless of whether his parent is always consistent. But a child of twelve, if he senses a lack of fair play, may well ask, "Why?" This is not to be construed as open rebellion necessarily, but simply as a reflection of his need to understand. Be willing to discuss it with him. Discipline must always be sensitive and well grounded.

The careful parent must consider the circumstances behind wrong behavior. Children occasionally have bad days. If a child is tired, for instance, that may provide a clue to his grumpiness. It won't necessarily justify the wrong, but it is a factor to consider before carrying out discipline.

Sometimes a child will feel he is worthless, that nothing is going right, that he is "out of sync" with life. Your response must take this into consideration. An act of selfishness may sometimes be a questioning of self-worth rather than an act of defiance. If the foundation of discipline has been well laid, a hug and some tender words to an angry child will not compromise it. And he will usually regain a positive feeling about himself much more easily than if he'd been taken on a trip to the woodshed.

You are responsible to provide conditions that help your child to mature. For a three-year-old toddler constantly asking, "Who's in charge?" your response must often be physical and painful. For the twelve-year-old girl experiencing the hormonal changes of adolescence, reassurance and a hug may be most helpful.

Older children are very sensitive about being forgiven. Parents are often reluctant to forgive their children but yet expect to be forgiven their own mistakes. This is clear from the readiness with which we punish for childish carelessness rather than for disobedience. Such constant cracking down for every little infraction forces the child to defend himself from parental assaults by using excuses, buck-passing, lying, etc. Consider the internal emotional influences before you lash out angrily—especially when his behavior involves some extenuating circumstance—or before you punish him for something he did not do. Each unfair and unloving word removes one tiny piece of trust from that relationship you hope to enjoy with him when he is an adult.

How much better when a child finds complete forgiveness in the arms of his parents. If he knows he can approach them any time, no matter what the offense, no matter what he has done, there will be few barriers to love and communication. Discipline will still be necessary. But in order for the child to properly sense guilt, he must first experience the love of compassionate parents and know that from the very first moment, forgiveness already exists in his parents' heart.

7. Training: Building Social Behavior, Skills, and Responsibility

If you maintain an idealistic vision of what you want your child to *become*, eventually you will be confronted with the reality of what your child *is*. How in the world are you going to transform that immature, sloppy, naive, uncoordinated little boy or girl into a mature, wise, radiant child of God?

There are seemingly hundreds of his behaviors which need to be shaped. Where and how do you start? How do you train him to function adequately in life's mundane affairs—to tie shoelaces, handle a knife and fork, dress himself, communicate with others, handle conflict, use money wisely, share, study efficiently, develop athletic and physical skills, carry out responsibility, understand his emotions, ride a bike, and hold down a job?

Don't become depressed at the immensity of the task. Be assured, YOU CAN DO IT!

Through discipline you aid in the formation of your child's attitudes which are reflected in his character. But, you also have to train your son or daughter to *do* things in the physical world. Though there is great overlap between discipline and training, they are not identical.

There are a number of methods you can use to steer your

89

child in a given direction. Of course you must know where you want him to go. But once that is decided (once you know that you want your child to say "please" and "thank you," to be able to cook, to be able to hold his own athletically, and be able to keep his room clean), you can apply those methods and teach any uncoordinated youngster to ride a bike, hit a ball, or make a dress; you can even teach a sloppy kid social graces; and you can turn impatience into self-control. It may not be easy, but it can be done.

When you're attempting to modify your child's behavior, at certain times he will be eager and willing to learn. Then your job is easy; the only thing you can do wrong is dampen his enthusiasm. But at other times he will not be so motivated, and he will not care about improving his conduct. He will be perfectly content to remain immature forever. At such times you will have to devise ways to induce him toward habits you desire him to have. Permanent changes can rarely be imposed on a child without his willingness. *Motivation* is the key. Since you as a parent are in control of many of his circumstances, there are many things you can do to manipulate his motivation and thus propel him toward the goals you have set.

The training methods discussed in this chapter will have varied uses; some will prove more useful when your child is 100% cooperative and others will help when you and he are at odds and you need "ammunition." But all are necessary, because children are constantly changing.

Conscious and Subconscious Instruction

Children respond to everything they hear. Therefore your child's personality and demeanor are fashioned by all you say. This takes place in two ways:

1. The most basic method for shaping a child's social behavior is through conscious instruction. Much of what he

learns to do, he learns by listening and then following instructions. In his younger years he enthusiastically hangs on your every word, anxious to do whatever you tell him.

2. Your words also have a subtle, subconscious impact. You are indirectly training your child all day long without realizing it. Your child hears your words even in your unguarded moments. The manner in which you express yourself will affect his view of the world and his internal habit patterns.

Obviously, the combination of direct verbal instruction and indirect subconscious training occur all day long. But you are usually only aware of the first. Therefore your child grows to reflect your patterns gradually—whether or not you desire it—simply because of the impact of your words.

If you want to fulfill your goals for your child, you must pay strict attention to the words that flow in your home. For example, they will learn to be thankful or ungrateful by the way you respond to him and to other people. He will learn courtesy or rudeness, humility or arrogance, just by absorbing what he hears.

Note the difference in the responses to everyday situations:

NEGATIVE	POSITIVE
"I'm sick of this weather!"	"Isn't it good of God to give us the weather we need today?"
"Get outta my way!"	"Excuse me, please."
"Stop that!"	"Please, don't do that again."
"These prices make me mad."	"It's expensive, but the Lord will provide."

"Darn that guy anyway."	"God bless him; he's doing the best he can."
"More potatoes!"	"Please pass the potatoes."
"Don't bother me now."	"I'm sorry, I don't have time just now."
"Your closet's a mess!"	"I think your closet could use a little work."
"Not bad. Could have been better."	"Hey, great job!"

Griping and complaining will develop an unthankful outlook on life in your child's heart. On the other hand, if you thank your husband for helping with the dishes or if you compliment your wife for the nice dinner, your child will be apt to have a positive, thankful outlook. Kind, complimentary, appreciative words will almost guarantee that similar speech will eventually flow from the lips of your child. A child uses the words he hears. He will adopt not only your words, but your mannerisms, idiosyncrasies, and attitudes. He will imitate both *what* you say and *how* you say it.

Imitation and Example

Real learning does not usually occur as a task is explained or even as it is demonstrated. Although explanation and demonstration are necessary, a child has to try something new *for himself*. He needs to get "the feel of it" with his own fingers and feet. For your words to have the most effect, you must provide practice with your teaching, allowing your child time to imitate you. For example, as you explain about tying a shoe, you must show him the process step-by-step, then let him practice each step.

Two factors make practice all the more effective. *Encouragement*, for one, is vital. Nothing will motivate him to learn faster than your support. Second, large tasks must be broken down into small enough increments that a child can master individually. The entire process might be overwhelming, but he can tackle small chunks successfully.

This process not only applies to physical skills such as tying shoes or riding bikes, but it also applies to social behavior. You can talk to your son or daughter about thankfulness, for instance. Your words instruct. The tone and manner of your speech establish a pattern he or she will imitate. Then you daily provide examples where thankfulness would be the suitable response. If your goal is to "have a thankful daughter," don't expect to accomplish that in one sitting. Rather, break the task down into manageable pieces and work on being thankful for today's hotcakes at breakfast, then praise and congratulate her for even the most feeble efforts. Thus she will be motivated to continue learning.

At this point behavior training takes a different route than the disciplinary training we discussed in the previous chapter. When instilling obedience you must often be firm and unbending, insisting on strict compliance. However, when teaching a new task, much leniency and patience are necessary. Your daughter will have a difficult time learning thankfulness if you never show appreciation for her efforts. Your son will hardly be motivated to learn to ride his new bike if every time he tries you criticize his every move. Nothing will dampen motivation faster than ungratefulness and criticism.

Your example is vital. So much of what a child acquires in personal habit patterns comes not so much through direct teaching but from observation and imitation of other family members. For example, a youngster learns to talk not by being lectured on how to speak but by being surrounded with words and grammar in use. His mind absorbs what is about him, assimilates it, and he then begins practicing on his own. His grammar will approximate the grammar used by the rest of the family.

As he grows, much of his behavior becomes part of his personality simple because his is immersed in your particular family. Many basic habit patterns are passed along to a child with no instruction or planning whatsoever. Depending on your awareness and care, this principle can either work for or against you.

Positive Reinforcement—Rewards

Many times a youngster would rather have nothing to do with what you want to teach him. A toddler would be content to eat with his fingers forever, but you know you must train him to use a fork and spoon. A preschooler would just as soon leave his room looking like a tornado had hit, but you recognize his need to learn orderliness. A sixth grader would rather play than do his homework. But being aware of his long-range need, you must take it upon yourself to teach him how to study and make sure he does study. A teen-ager would rather be out with friends than working on his chores or fulfilling his obligation at a part-time job. So it is your duty to see that he learns responsibility in these matters.

No child wants to clean his room, pull weeds, do his schoolwork, pick up the garage, or sweep the patio when he can play instead. But you know training him to responsibly carry out such small tasks insures that in later years he will be able to function in the world with integrity, responsibility, and maturity.

There are a number of techniques you can employ to increase a child's self-motivation and to mold his behavior, though at first he may be an unwilling learner. The most important of these is the use of rewards. If a child is rewarded for something he has done, he will want to do it again. This can either help or hinder your intentions. When your son receives a big hug and a word of praise for helping with the yard work, he will want to help again—you have set a pattern of helpfulness in motion. But if your two-year-old daughter has her tantrum rewarded by your surrendering to her demands, she will undoubtedly try kicking and screaming again in the future—you may have initiated a habit that could plague you for years.

The most effective rewards are not candy, presents, or second helpings of pie, but rather praise, affirmation, and appreciation. However, once you have built a strong base of love and acceptance, you can skillfully offer more tangible incentives as well. If you are training your son to trim the edge of the lawn and rake up the clippings, his internal motivation may at first be low, but your praise will be something he will want to earn again and again. This forms the foundation. Once he begins to willingly perform his tasks, you may add such inducements as a snack together after the job is completed, money for a movie, or something else which he desires.

Timing is also important. Several days later the emotional energy of having helped you clean the garage will be gone. Praise at that point will not have much impact. If given immediately while the child is still feeling an emotional charge from the job (most tasks are not purely physical but involve the emotional being), he will experience a great boost. As children grow older, they become increasingly capable of thinking about the future. Older children, therefore, can be motivated through the use of long-range goals. A family's banding together to drink powdered milk for the purpose of saving money toward a family trip or a new trampoline is an example of a long-term motivation.

Rewards must be *positive*. They should not be given for *not* doing something bad but for *doing* something good. Rewarding what your child *doesn't* do subtly reinforces the negative behavior, even if in reverse. Therefore, reward your thirteen-year-old for having a *tidy* room (positive thrust) rather than for not having a *sloppy* room (negative thrust). The difference seems minor at first glance, but backwards rewarding insures that the negative behavior will continue since it provides the basis for the reward.

Negative Reinforcement/Extinction

A behavior that goes unrewarded will eventually die out. If you are trying to rid your child of some annoying habit, this is the ideal tool. If, for example, you are trying to stop your youngster from making certain demands on you, don't fulfill his selfish requests.

We often unconsciously prolong bad habits rather than extinguish them. At 5 p.m., Dad walks in the door after an exasperating day at work. Four-year-old Joey asks for a cookie and is denied. He unleashes a tantrum. Mom is fixing dinner and has a headache. Dad hardly has his coat off and is in no mood to hear screaming for 45 minutes until dinner, so he grudgingly gives Joey a cookie. "Just this once," he warns, with little conviction. Joey doesn't mind. He has observed that his request, when followed by a tantrum, brought results. The next time he wants his own way he will probably use the same method. His screaming has been reinforced.

If Dad is the emotional sort and has just had to deal with a cranky superior before leaving work, his response might be different. Junior's tantrum might then be met with an explosion of rage and a spanking. The screaming, of course, continues and now everyone has a headache.

But if Mom and Dad refuse to reward Joey's demands and screaming spells, he will *gradually* learn there are more effective means to achieve results than throwing himself headlong on the floor (*if* Mom and Dad are alertly rewarding pleasant behavior). Ignoring tantrums will usually help reduce them but offering bribes ("I'll give you this piece of candy if you'll just stop.") will insure their continuation.

This extinction process can also produce negative effects. An insensitive parent may ignore his child's good behavior and helpful habits and never dish out a single word of praise. Ultimately the good habits will die out. A cooperative and obedient child who receives little attention from his father may seek alternate ways to gain recognition. If he discovers that writing on the walls with a crayon and testing the scissors on the living-room curtains wins his father's attention (though it may be in the form of a spanking), he may well continue such pranks. His good behavior has gone unnoticed while his new recklessness is regularly reinforced.

Reinforcement and extinction should be practiced constantly and carefully. Most parents have no idea of the extent to which they unconsciously reward their child both positively and negatively. When used with awareness, however, these tools can be very useful in motivating your child toward acceptable behavior.

Reasoning and Communication

The older your child grows the more you will be able to reason with him and help him train himself. Communication is a prerequisite for preventing problems with a son or daughter. Discussion of misbehavior in a mature rather than hostile manner ("This is why such-and-such isn't appropriate." "But, Dad, I don't really understand this.") opens the way for a stronger relationship between you and your child. Of course your authority must always be evident. But discussing the pros and cons of a weekend curfew and agreeing on a mutually acceptable solution (without your having to heavy-handedly exercise your authority) will increase your child's respect for you.

Dialogue can lead a child into new areas of learning and understanding. When you and your child are communicating, when he senses you are trying to understand him, he is able to perceive things more clearly. This requires sensitivity and attentive listening. It means allowing him to express even negative opinions freely. When he knows he can unleash his feelings without fear of reprisal, his emotions can mature properly. You must respect him and feel *with* him. When he hurts, much of his relief will come from knowing you hurt, too.

"Conversational feedback" is one technique for helping a child understand his emotions. As you speak to him, restate the emotions your child has expressed. Rather than offering advice at every step, simply feed back to him what you perceive his feelings to be. He is thus encouraged to think further until, through your gentle guidance, he comes to understand his problem.

Restating your child's expression does two important things: it shows you have heard him—and that you care, *and* it provides a springboard to further discussion.

For example, your thirteen-year-old daughter storms into the house after school, obviously disgusted. "Boy, I'm mad at Lisa for what she did today!" she says with a growl.

You have three choices. You can piously sermonize, "You know, honey, a Christian shouldn't be angry with her friends," in which case your daughter will probably clam up and sulk in her room until dinnertime. She will quickly learn not to share her feelings with you. (This does not mean there is no place for spiritual counsel, but timing is critical.)

You can instead say, "Why? What happened?" This

would be much better because at least you present yourself as a neutral observer rather than as a critical parent.

If you respond with, "I can tell you are upset and frustrated. Lisa must have done something really bad," you are accomplishing something far greater. You have now actively involved yourself in your daughter's emotions. You have not just heard what she said, you have *felt* it with her. You are not just casually responding as you take a break from your dinner preparations, but you are placing yourself in the midst of her feelings. (Don't say, "I understand what you mean. . . ," but express sincerely the emotions she has just shared.)

Your daughter may then respond, "I couldn't believe what she said to me! And I'm supposed to be her best friend!"

"She really lashed out at you, huh? Her own best friend?"

"It wasn't like her at all."

"No, it doesn't sound like what I know of her. It must have really hurt you. There must've been something on her mind to make her treat you like that."

Communication is taking place. There is no pressure, no critical glare. Your daughter senses that you have plunged into this little crisis with her. Such communication can motivate her to change her attitude. Such a change could probably not come by telling her, "You ought to. . . " Advice is often the least appropriate thing to offer. She needs to be motivated from within.

Finally, she admits, "Yeah, I guess there has been something on her mind. She's been acting a little moody all week. I've tried to cheer her up a few times, but nothing seems to help."

"I'm glad you've tried to help."

"I probably didn't do as much as I could. She's my best friend, so I suppose I should try to help more."

"That's what best friends are for, to ease each other's burdens when the going gets rough."

"Yeah. Now I feel bad for getting mad at her."

"What do you suppose you ought to do about it?"

"Maybe I ought to call her. Maybe she'd tell me what's wrong. What do you think, Mom?"

"That sounds like a nice thing to do. It would show Lisa you really care."

"I do. She's a good friend."

"Why don't we pray for her before you call?"

"Okay—thanks, Mom."

Results won't always come so visibly and quickly as in this example. And if you expect a quick response, your child will sense the pressure. Your motive must not necessarily be to get him to come around to your point of view, but to understand his feelings. When you do, his self motivation will take over, though not necessarily in ways you'd expect.

Habit Formation

We each form hundreds of habits; routine is a key part of our existence. Without a tenacious effort by parents, however, children establish undesirable habits. You must decide what habit patterns you want your children to have, for *good* habits can orient a child toward godly behavior. If you are always trying to cope with situations, you will always be one step behind, trying to undo already formed habits. It takes serious planning to forge new habits where none existed previously. You need a strategy that can mold and control events and bring dynamic new patterns into your child's life!

What a challenge!

Many of your child's habits will be based on the way you order your home. But many habits need to be taught deliberately. Toilet training, table manners, speech patterns, sleeping through the night, playing with friends, curbing anger, and speaking respectfully are all matters of habit. Without bold guidance from parents, a child will acquire whatever habits—many of them negative—happen to settle into his personality. It is no wonder parents have a difficult time altering undesirable behavior when their children are older. The habits are already ingrained deeply. If you want *good* habits in *your* child, you must see that they are formed right the *first* time. Reforming habits later is nearly impossible.

Habits are formed by repetition. If a child clears his section of the dinner table, takes the dishes to the sink, and receives praise for his work, he will undoubtedly try it again. If the encouragement continues, he will keep on clearing his portion of the table. If this pattern is maintained long enough, a habit will form. Through conscientious use of rewards and praise, a parent can instill the helpful habit of clearing the table.

Any habit can be formed or broken in this manner. If a poor habit goes unrewarded, you can cause it to gradually die out. If you do not praise a good habit, it too will ultimately cease. If you are not paying attention to what habits your children are developing, they will gain poor habits and lose good ones due to your neglect.

When working on a habit, a large range of considerations comes into play. Simply teaching a child to ride a bicycle can illustrate nearly all the tools mentioned in this chapter. There is the initial *instruction* and dialogue. Then he must try it for himself. It requires much *practice*. He needs *encouragement* to keep going. You praise him and he feels the thrill and satisfaction of going fifteen feet on his own. There is, perhaps painfully, a *natural consequence* to failure—the crash at the end of the line. You may need to instruct further. Eventually, with enough practice, he learns to ride skillfully. A habit has formed that will last a lifetime.

In our home we shift around methods and rewards to maintain a sense of newness. Sometimes we reward instantly with snacks. Perhaps a kind word or a shared toy will receive a peanut. These are motivational gimmicks to be sure, but they keep attention and interest high. Older children will require different applications of the reward/reinforcement principle. Teaching good sportsmanship, for example, has a less tangible long-range consequence for failure—loss of respect from other children. Therefore, to instill the habit of losing graciously will require a creative approach. But whatever your child's age and whatever habits you are working on, *the example of your own actions and attitudes* will be your most effective tool.

For several months my wife and I determined to help our sons develop the habit of gracious speech. Our boys had been picking up negative speech patterns we wanted to break. We recognized that certain words and tones bred certain attitudes; "Get out of my way!" conveys an air of self-importance and shows disrespect to other people.

By focusing on the "nice" ways of saying things, we hoped to eliminate the problem of brash inconsiderateness revealed by their words. We introduced our boys to such phrases as "would you please," "may I please," "would it be all right with you," and reaffirmed the importance of "thank you" and other polite expressions. We taught them to substitute "Would it be all right with you if I used that ball?" for, "I want that ball." At every opportunity we discussed the difference between:

| "Stop it" | vs. | "Would you mind not doing that?" |
| "I want" | vs. | "May I please have . . . ?" |

"Hey, outta my way!" vs. "Pardon me please. May I get through?"

Once we had introduced the idea, we had to somehow make them want to change their habits and use polite expressions. So we drew a large chart of squares, and every polite phrase we heard was instantly rewarded with a star in a square. When a row of five was completed, there was a peanut waiting. A full chart won an 89¢ dime store trinket of their choice.

There were rewards every few seconds it sometimes seemed—first the star, then the peanut, then the final prize. They were stimulated by the different levels of rewards and worked hard to invent new phrases. Sometimes they were so clever that two or three stars would follow each other in rapid succession.

No matter how artificial the phrase sounded, we rewarded it. We were busy not only putting up stars but drawing new charts to replace the filled ones. We rejoiced because we could see the habits forming from sheer repetition. The boys sounded more polite, and the whole atmosphere of our home seemed gradually to transform. Our boys were no longer offensively shouting out orders, but they were politely speaking to Judy and me, their friends, and adults. Before long the polite phrases became second nature to them.

The charts and rewards absorbed less of their interest as time passed because the intensity of their efforts decreased. But the habit patterns were formed. It then became a matter of maintaining it with periodic work. We were then able to move on to other areas of concentration and the polite speech continued.

The transformation didn't take place through magic. It was a result of planning, determination, and hard work.

Giving Responsibility

A child is often motivated to raise his performance level when given some new responsibility—a challenge which will stretch him beyond his present capabilities without being impossible. Parents who respect their child's abilities will give him new duties that stimulate him to excell, to learn, to exert himself, and to succeed. One of your prime objectives as a parent should be to gradually place your child's affairs on his own shoulders. You are working to produce a capable adult. You can do so one step at a time by sensitively increasing your child's responsibility for his life while lessening your own. The process must move slowly, however; too much too soon can cause a tender youngster to crack from the pressure.

Related closely to this is the need to learn dependability. Once the motivational "high" of being given a new assignment wears off, a child will naturally want to be relieved from it. At that point he needs to follow through. This is not easy, for diligence is not innate; it comes from practice. Haim Ginott comments:

> Children are not born with a built-in sense of responsibility. Neither do they acquire it automatically at a certain prescribed age. Responsibility, like piano playing, is attained slowly and over many years. It requires daily practice (encouragement and experiences) in exercising judgment and in making choices about matters appropriate to one's age and comprehension. . . .[11]

Once he is an adult there will be no one to bail him out when he tires of his vocation. He needs to learn long-term dependability through the smaller doses of increasing childhood tasks.

Suppose your son wants a paper route or a new dog, or your daughter wants to take an after-school job at an alterations shop. You should use that desire for his benefit and teach him to faithfully carry out the obligations inherent in the job. When the time comes (and it certainly will) when he is hesitant to deliver papers in the rain, or tires of feeding the dog twice a day, or when she resists when called by the employer for a rush job because her friends are gathered for an afternoon together, you cannot allow them to shirk the responsibility accepted earlier. If he/she is unwilling to follow through, the consequence must be to give up the paper route, the dog, or the job. You cannot intervene between your child and his responsibility if you expect him to become a dependable adult.

You must show great leniency when your child first begins assuming responsibility. He will have a difficult time. Learning to be trusted with difficult assignments is a progressive thing. When teaching your three-year-old to carry his own clothes upstairs to his dresser, you will be far more tolerant and less demanding of results than you will when expecting your twelve-year-old to keep his room clean. You cannot expect a child to be more responsible than his age allows. But by the time he is fourteen or fifteen, he should be able to accept accountability for many of his actions. Children whose parents fail to instill such responsibility in early life will have a difficult time as adults.

In seventh grade I accepted a gardening job at a neighbor's home which would require several afternoons a week. It was one of my first exposures to a long-term job, and I had to carry it out whether or not I liked it. There were times when I would rather have been involved in some attractive after-school activity. On several occasions I would have ducked out of my responsibility if I'd found a way. Thankfully my parents recognized my need to learn diligence through that job and kept after me. My present attitude toward my own business had many of its roots in that early experience.

Self-discipline, an element of responsibility, is a necessary ingredient for a successful, balanced life. You can help your child acquire self-discipline in two significant ways:

1. *By teaching responsibility in the daily affairs of the home*—wise spending, household chores, proper care of possessions, decision-making.

2. *By showing interest in his performance.* Giving encouragement, occasionally sharing duties and giving him a temporary break when necessary will help to maintain your child's motivation. Responsibility must be heavy enough to require a conscientious effort, but don't allow it to become an excessive burden. Don't expect your son or daughter to have the stamina of an adult—yet!

Natural Consequences

If you are unsuccessfully trying to rid your youngster of a bad habit, you can sometimes correct it by doing nothing at all—by allowing the natural consequences to intervene. If there will be mildly unpleasant effects from his actions, your tendency will be to shield him from them. DON'T! Let him face the consequences and don't offer protection.

The father of the prodigal son in Luke 15 used this method of training. He did not tell his son, "You need to grow up!" Even though there was a certain amount of stubbornness and rebellion in this young man's heart, his father recognized his need to learn and mature by facing the natural results of his desired life-style. So he let him go. And his son later returned home with a transformed attitude.

You may be attempting to teach your toddler not to rub his eyes when washing with soap. But no matter what you say he continues to try. Why not let him face the consequences of his actions? Let him rub his eyes. They will sting but he won't suffer any real injury. His own actions will bring an end to this habit soon enough.

Finicky eating can be cured in the same way. Rather than catering to a child's refusal to eat by giving snacks and cooking preferred foods, a parent can simply allow hunger to take its course. There is nothing like a few missed meals to strengthen the appetite.

Of course good sense must be used with this approach. It is clearly inappropriate to teach a child to be careful with fire, to swim, or to overcome fear of heights by using this method. A child must not be placed in danger. If hazards exist, use other tools.

Logical Consequences

Logical consequences are similiar to natural ones. But instead of allowing *nature* to determine the outcome, *you* as a parent engineer a logical result for the behavior you would like to eliminate. If he is to finish a chore by a given hour, then go out and play, the logical outcome of not completing it would be to miss the playtime. If he cannot remember to take his lunch, Dad should not drop it off at the school office on his way to work. The logical consequences of forgetfulness is simple—no lunch that day.

Teaching through both natural and logical consequences will motivate effectively. By having to assume the repercussions of his own actions, a child will alter his behavior so that the outcome benefits his own best interests. If he is constantly protected from unpleasant side-effects, he won't have this opportunity.

The use of logical consequences must not become a parent's excuse for a disinterested hands-off relationship. A parent must not become too busy to discover what is best for his child. These techniques must be used like all the others in this and the previous chapter—with thoughtful planning. Because consequences are logical and natural does not imply we should let them occur at random. They must be carefully integrated into a total training program.

Other Training Techniques

Two other effective techniques you may need are *isolation* and *deprivation*. Misbehavior or bad habits you want to correct can sometimes be extinguished by isolating a child from everyone else, especially those his actions are directed against. If the child is placed in seclusion, often the habit can be forced to die out. Once his intended victims are gone, there ceases to be any purpose in continuing—no one is listening or watching.

Isolation can be creatively applied in many situations. Some parents find it successful in combating tantrums. If the goal of the tantrum is to compel a haggard parent to submit to a demand, the child should be sent to his room. When his parents no longer hear his screaming, he quits.

In our family, however, we have successfully dealt with tantrums through deprivation—taking away something that is meaningful—as a consequence to their screaming. We have withheld meals upon occasion to punish unsociable behavior. It is a radical measure—downright shocking the first time it happens to an unsuspecting youngster! But, with our children at least, it grabbed their attention in a hurry. The next time they were tempted to break loose with arms, legs, and vocal cords, they had second thoughts.

So many things are perfectly suited for this deprivation—TV, dessert, a Saturday activity, allowances, etc. Of course you must be consistent and loving, and not applying these punishments angrily or impetuously. But if used as part of a unified effort to train a child in positive ways, deprivation as well as isolation can be very helpful techniques.

Deciding Which Technique to Use

Many of these techniques work side-by-side. Rarely does one used alone completely clear up a problem, instill a wonderfully positive habit, or train a child to behave in a given way. Usually one particular method will prove especially suitable in a given circumstance, but secondary techniques may combine with it to do the job more thoroughly. Your task—a difficult one—is to find which tools to use when faced with a dilemma in your home.

The key is sensitivity—to your child's feelings, needs, attitudes, maturity, abilities and potential. You may not always recognize one technique as the appropriate one to use. You may have to experiment to find what will work. If you are genuinely sensitive to your child's needs, he will not be hurt by such uncertainties.

Generally you will want to progress from the most gentle to the most harsh techniques. For example, if it becomes time to train your child to take care of toys, tools, bikes, etc., you would first talk about it. You would reason with him, instructing him about caring for his possessions. In some cases this might be enough.

However, one day you may notice that he is not caring for his bicycle. Soon you observe a general sloppiness setting in. You will need to correct this growing negative habit with a more deeply instilled positive one. You and your spouse must then devise a system of rewards (a chart or certain privileges or some sort of material incentive) to motivate him to nightly put his bike in the garage. You are aware that the repetition of positive behavior will cement a good pattern into place. You are also aware that your own example of caring for your possessions is also working in your son's consciousness.

Possibly the rewards produce the desired result. What if they don't? Then you begin to implement more stringent consequences on your son's inappropriate behavior. Thus, one night, when he leaves his bike in the yard, you do not remind him of it. The next morning he prepares to ride to school and finds his bike wet with dew—the natural consequence of his forgetfulness. If this happens very many times, the bike will begin to rust. If he is responsible for the cost of maintaining the bicycle, he will pay an increasingly heavy price for his own mistakes.

If natural consequences do not work, you will have to be more extreme. When later in the school year he asks for a new football, you might have to say, "I'm really sorry, son. I just can't buy you a football until you properly care for the things you already have. You're still leaving your bike out at night. I'd like for you to have the ball, but to me it's even more important that you learn diligence. When I see some progress with the bike, we'll talk about the football."

Now your son is "cornered." His carelessness is coming back to haunt him. Hopefully before too much longer he will take action and start putting the bike away.

There do come times, however, when all these methods fail to achieve results, and you should suspect there is a deeper problem than the need for behavioral training. When *attitude* is at the root of the problem, discipline is needed.

Discipline and training can overlap in certain situations. It is sometimes necessary to use spanking to teach behavior. You obviously cannot train your 18-month-old about the stove or to stay on the sidewalk by reasoning with him. But even though in the daily situations you face there will be much overlap, you need to keep discipline and training separate in your thinking to apply them wisely.

This will not be easy!

In teaching your three-year-old to dress himself, your seven-year-old to take care of his books, and your eleven-year-old to carry out his household jobs, you will be training in the arena of behavior and you will be dealing with resistant attitudes which sometimes oppose your teaching. The older your children grow the more intertwined all these factors become. But the various tools still must not be confused. You may use logical consequences to instill responsibility and at the same time spank your child for an attitude of defiance. But you must have it clear in your mind that you are not spanking him because he filled up on snacks after school and now won't eat his dinner, but rather because he disobeyed and gave you "back talk" in the process. In order to motivate him toward more mature eating habits, you also need to employ a behavioral tool.

There will be times you won't know exactly which area you are dealing with. If you tell your daughter to be home at five o'clock and she wanders in at five-thirty, there has surely been disobedience. But are you dealing with open rebellion or simple childish irresponsibility? Disobedience is not always rebellion, nor does following instructions to the letter always signal a submissive heart attitude. You must know your child well, be full of love and ask God for wisdom. Every situation will be different.

A child may disobey and to all appearances it may seem you are dealing with a rebellious attitude. But he may actually be trying to gain your attention. His disobedience may not call for disciplinary tools at all, but a change in your schedule which allows you more time with him.

What appears to be a bad attitude may in fact be erupting emotional frustrations which are being released by yelling, hitting, and screaming. Coming down hard could set in motion trends of non-acceptance and guilt. What he might need is the freedom to find acceptance just as he is.

Although having made such a point of this distinction between behavior and attitude, I must add that as a child grows older, in certain ways this distinction begins to fade away. Once a scriptural basis for authority has been laid in the early years, discipline can begin to be carried out using some of the behavioral tools.

The parent of every teen-ager knows all about the use of deprivation for disobedience. Young adults must learn proper attitudes the hard way—through logical and natural consequences and by having to face up to increasing responsibilities. It is obviously unwise to physically spank your fifteen-year-old son for a problem attitude (spanking should probably be gradually drawn to a close between 8 and 11). But if in that child's early years a strong foundation has been laid, you can now employ other tools and achieve results.

Your success in doing this will be a direct result of the effectiveness and consistency of your earlier discipline and training. The gradual process of increasing the use of behavioral tools for disciplinary purposes is a slow one. It takes place over several years as children grow beyond the spanking age. The more independent they become, the more you can see they are responsible for their own actions *and* attitudes.

8. Raising Godly Men and Women Through Prayer

The subconscious mind plays a key role in the development of a child's self-image. Therefore my prayer time with my boys (after they are asleep) goes beyond just making my requests for them known to God. I kneel by their bedsides and talk, not only to God but to *them* as well. I use the time for prayer *and* for revealing to their subconscious minds the vision I have for each of them.

I quietly tell them (while they're asleep) those very things I try to stress to their conscious minds throughout the day: "You are a good boy. You are unselfish. You are my friend. You are skilled. I'm proud to call you my son." I know my words reach them, for I occasionally receive sleepy whispered responses. Nearly every night I tell them, "You are God's boy. God is making you into one of His men. God loves you and has chosen you for a special purpose. He's going to use you to tell people about Him." Sometimes they have nodded their heads and given nearly inaudible reactions. Their subconsciouses bypass the conscious mind and respond!

But saying things to them, as important as that is, will only have a limited effect. I also voice those desires and ambitions to God on their behalf. This allows God to effect results far beyond what I could ever accomplish. As I pray I perceive my role to be like a young boy with a magnifying glass, trying to focus the sun's rays to ignite a scrap of paper. The power is all in the sun, but the boy positions the glass and thus taps the available power. When I pray, I focus the "glass" so that God's power can penetrate their young lives.

I pray as specifically as possible. A vague, "shotgun" approach—"Lord, bless Patrick tonight and work your will into his life"—is better than no prayer at all. But if I concentrate God's love and power on particular areas of their lives the results will be much greater.

First I pray for specific needs that may have arisen that day. If there has been a fall, some sickness or emotional bruise, I pray for both physical and emotional healing. If there are some problems with his schoolwork or with a friend, or if he is having a bout with insecurity, I present that to the Lord. I also tell the Lord about those areas in which I feel inadequate to meet the needs of that son.

If there has been some trauma, I pray for healing of his memories. This is no different than praying for physical healing. You can simply ask God to heal you son's (or daughter's) memory of his bicycle accident, the dog bite, being laughed at in school, his uncle's terminal illness which he cannot understand, or his getting lost on the way home from the store. You do not necessarily ask God to give him amnesia regarding the matter, but ask Him to remove the intense pain in his emotions caused by the memory.

Jesus can act as an emotional lightning rod. Potential hurts will move from your child's experience into his subconscious where they can continue to plague him. Jesus can intercept them and "ground" them into himself. You and I cannot do this for our children because we cannot enter a person's mind. But Jesus can keep the memory from permanently implanting itself in the inner being.

You are like a computer programmer. If healing is required to right an incorrect "program" that has been entered, you as the programmer must diagnose the problem and present it to God for healing. You pray for God to "erase" the negative program at that precise point of hurt in your child's memory. You ask Him to replace the negative emotional memory with a positive one instead. However you choose to look at the process, or whatever you wish to call it, God *is* able to provide wholeness through prayer of this kind.

Then I cover more general areas of concern in my prayer—long-term concerns and specific things I hope to build into his life.

"Lord, I ask you to make this boy completely yours. Wrap your arms around him. Cover him with your care. Send your guardian angels to minister to him and watch over him. Fill him with your Spirit. Make him sensitive, kind, obedient, respectful, unselfish and submissive. Develop those qualities in my life as well so that he has a model of godliness to imitate. Give him an inner awareness of how special he is, of how much you love him and of how much I love him. May he grow up to know, love and serve you. Enlarge within his heart a deepening desire to know you and obey you in all things.

"I pray for his future. I dedicate him to serve you. Be especially near him at those crucial moments of life when he needs to make major decisions. I pray for that moment of opportunity when he is standing at the crossroads facing the choice of whether or not to give his life to you. Prepare him for that moment. Place a spark in his young heart now that will flame up and will at that time illuminate the truth to him. Draw him into eternal fellowship with you.

"Throughout his life provide him with the people he needs. I pray for his future wife, friends, associates, teachers, and counselors. I pray for all those who are influenced by his life. I pray for his future sons and daughters. Prepare him to minister to them and to love them deeply.

Prepare him to be a strong and loving husband and father. Instill within him these same urgent commitments that are burning in my own heart for the family.

"I pray that in my personal relationship with him, we will be able to build something permanent, something that will affect eternally the future generations of this family and all whom they touch. Place within him the desire to build into his own children far greater things than I can even imagine, and teach them to build into their children as well.

"Somehow, Lord, compensate for my mistakes and short-sightedness. Increase my commitment to this boy I love so much. Help me to heed my own words and to keep my priorities in balance. Keep me from getting too busy. Bridge the gap between his needs and my human weaknesses. Fill Judy and me with your wisdom. Give us patience and sensitivity to serve him more effectively. Protect him, Lord, and keep him close to your heart."

Finally, I focus my thoughts and prayers on the spiritual battle being waged against my son. I pray for God's protection on him. As the authority over my family and my sons, I bind the power of Satan and his spirits in the name of Jesus. I cover my sons by faith with the cleansing and protecting blood of Jesus. I pray for God to surround him with a hedge of protection from the forces in the world that counter His principles and all that I would build into my family. And I pray also for myself and my wife, that the Lord would protect us and keep us in His will. I pray that He would preserve the umbrella of our authority over our sons, keeping it intact and effective. I ask God to make us wise, strong, and able to do battle against Satan, his fallen angels, and the world.

With three boys to pray for I don't nightly pray this completely for each one. I pray for the needs that are particularly evident in each of their lives. But over the weeks and months all the "bases" are covered and prayed about.

9. Preparing Your Child for the Future

Whatever you try to teach your child must be exemplified in your life. If he has observed consistency in his parents, when the world taunts, "Forget those outdated values your parents taught you—they're primitive and unenlightened," he will be able to stand fast. He will be able to say, "I won't leave them. I've seen those values lived out in my parents' lives, and I know they work." The most important ingredient in preparing your child for the future is *not* family field trips or marvelous training techniques but *your character.*

A Parental Model Gives a Child Strength

Leadership in a family hinges on the father, though of course a wife complements her husband's role. God has called the man to guide his children into maturity, into the full potential God intends for them. Every moment of the relationship between a child and his father contributes to the maturing process. A boy wearing his father's shoes is symbolic of a deep emotional and spiritual desire. That boy wants more than anything to emulate his father. And chances are—he will!

Children usually become what their parents are. All you

are as a man or woman is slowly being ingrained into their budding characters. Occasionally being on your best behavior won't condition your children properly. They learn dignity, honesty, compassion, and respect only by witnessing such qualities in their parents and siblings.

One of my most enjoyable pastimes is running. It has taught me something about being a father. In a road race of ten kilometers, if one runner happens to be heavily favored, he sets the tempo for the others. He doesn't necessarily occupy the lead from start to finish, but because of his reputation the others recognize him as the pacesetter. The pace he dictates is emotional as well as physical. He is the acknowledged leader. The others are aware of his pace no matter where in the pack he momentarily happens to be. And when the runners approach the finish line, he usually has gained a sizeable lead.

So it is with a father's role. He is not constantly with his family. He is generally gone during much of the day. Yet if he is a dynamic leader, a strong model for his child, he will be setting the pace even in his absence. He influences the quality of the family life and its direction. Unfortunately, a poor father-model will also set the pace, although toward an undesirable end.

Because of his frequent absence, a father must be highly aware of the importance of his time at home. Because of television, today's youngster can easily acquire much of his value system from the world. The father, therefore, must tenaciously retain the right to determine what will influence his child. He must freely expose his character, his integrity, his attitudes, and his emotions to his child.

The relationship between a father and mother is so important. A child is keenly perceptive of the sort of marriage that binds his parents. Everything that flows between them is observed. Disagreements, affection, and helpfulness are all on display. The child will "file" the input he gains from his parents' relationship and then apply it to his own future marriage.

Parents Are Leaders

Effective leaders do not accomplish their goals haphazardly. They plan, prepare, and diligently pursue those goals. The pursuit of goals has to be applied to the moment-by-moment problems that arise. This is a parent's twofold job—to cope with the immediate *and* to work toward the future; to set policy *and* to carry it out. It is a job no executive would have the fortitude to tackle, for unlike the businessman, the parent has no one to expedite his policy decisions for him. The parent is both the policy-making executive *and* the hard-working subordinate who carries it through.

Concerned parents must train themselves to function on two levels—in the busyness of day-to-day affairs and in the consciousness of long-range goals for their child. A child will not "turn out okay" unless there is a plan of action being implemented through effective parental leadership.

Many of today's fathers are weak-kneed leaders. Often they don't lead at all, so the mother takes command. Soon the family structure is confused. Children develop an unbiblical perspective of family order. If you are a father and don't feel like a leader, don't be terrified. Most people aren't born leaders—but they can choose to develop leadership capabilities. God will give grace!

Until this century, families in our country lived in an agrarian society where parental leadership was more visible. A rural family worked *together* throughout the day. The father was *there*; he did not say good-bye to his children each morning. They observed his life all day long. The various family relationships did not start and stop.

A few years ago I worked with a German farm family for six months. From 6 a.m. to 6 p.m. we all worked side-by-

"Here is what we want to accomplish in Johnny's life. Here is how we see him by faith."

Parents must, like executives, plan their goals for their child—

and then implement their plan in the day-to-day grind of life in the home.

side—father, mother, two older teen-agers, a son-in-law, an aunt, and myself. Though we often worked on separate jobs on different parts of the farm, there was a constant intertwining of relationships. The father ambitiously set the pace at all times.

Several advantages emerged from such constant family

interaction. There was sustained leadership by the father. The mother did not have to assume a dual role during the day. The children observed their parents in a wide variety of circumstances—their parents were strong models for them. The home was the undisputed center of life, for everyone.

In today's American society this is not usually true. As a child grows, the school replaces the home as his center of activity. The father's place of work is the center of his world. A father is most productive during the daytime hours, but he must give that time to his job rather than his child. He has minimal opportunity to demonstrate his life to him. The mother, if she doesn't have another job, is the only person, besides a preschool child, whose life revolves around the home.

Home life has therefore become leisure-oriented, a place to relax after the workday and to gear up for another day at the office, factory, or school. Most creative accomplishments, for the first grader or his father, are made outside the home. Much of the home's and family's significance is therefore lost.

We must take a fresh look at the purpose of our homes. The home should be the center for the *best* hours of the day and the most creative activities. A child won't thrive on leftover times. He needs the most exciting chunks of his parents' lives.

Control Your Child's Expanding Environment

A parent will not be taken by surprise if he is constantly watching for trends and problems in his child's behavior. He must spot tendencies even before the child himself is aware of them. An effective parent must learn to discriminate between healthy and unhealthy influences. He must make sure that his youngster continues to develop according to the plan he has made.

Worldly and satanic forces are constantly working to contaminate your child's motives and values. You will not counter these pressures with half-hearted, occasional spiritual input. You must be forceful. You must often act as a shield, warding off what is harmful. The poisoned arrows of ungodly attitudes will be flying at him from all directions. Your most difficult assignment is to ease him into the world without being infected by these dangerous darts.

You have been given responsibility for your child's growth. You are to control the progress of his expanding view of the world, of his relationships, and of himself. You are to provide an environment which contributes to his long-range development.

My wife and I have devoted ourselves to this task. We are keenly aware of each of our sons' strengths, weaknesses, and needs. From experience we have learned when to challenge them to move out and when to shield them from what we consider negative influences. We have visualized clear objectives for them and have made plans for reaching those goals. We expand the horizons of their world slowly. We push them outward at the moments when it will be most beneficial for them. Certain influences would undermine, perhaps destroy, the values and behaviors we are building into them. Therefore we do not allow them to confront anything which is out of our control unless its impact will be positive.

We have talked with some parents who maintain that such a stance will not adequately prepare our sons for the pressures of the world they must inevitably face. By so shielding him, they suggest, we will make them incapable of dealing with those things. They should, instead, be thrust out early. They claim overprotection creates an artificial environment which will only increase their susceptibility to the world.

I take the opposite view. We are, as Christians, trying to

produce a unique sort of person, unlike anything a non-Christian can understand. We are part of a grand adventure—training up godly men and women in the midst of a hostile world. Everything around us opposes that purpose. Therefore, our children must gain solid foundations in the safety of their home. There God's principles can be allowed to permeate their sensitive young minds. Once these principles have crystalized, they can capably confront and resist the onslaught of the world's values.

Most of us never realize the daily number of assaults on our children's minds. They are blasted incessantly by influences that shape their attitudes and values. TV, store displays, cereal boxes, billboards, playmates, neighbors, teachers, movies, radio, music, baby-sitters, Sunday-school teachers, conversations, magazines—all are bombarding their minds. Though such things each leave only slight impressions, the combined effect is staggering.

Most parents will shrug their shoulders at the idea and let their youngsters absorb whatever comes at him. *The Christian parent must do otherwise.* It's obviously impossible to keep all such influences out. But the Christian parent, concerned about giving his child a firm foundation, must diligently fight the negative influences. He must not allow the random flow of the world's values to mold his child. He must maintain a vigil against these messages that knock on the door of a child's mind. He must always ask, "Does this contribute toward or detract from the character I am trying to build in him?"

Then he must take appropriate action. For example, my wife and I purposely keep our boys from a number of neighborhood children. We have watched the children in our area and have concluded that some of them would damage our sons' character development. Their family values, discipline, play habits, language, and attitudes toward authority contradict the very things we desire to build into our boys. We scrutinize every potential relationship they have—church, school, family, and neighborhood friendships—to determine if the influence will be positive. We shield our boys from people we feel do not uphold the values we cherish, and we encourage those friendships we consider helpful for attaining our goals.

We have analyzed their school from the same perspective. We did not simply send our boys to the public school when the time came. We spent a couple of years assessing whether public or Christian school (or no school at all until age 8 or 9) would be best, when to enroll them in school, whether to send them to pre-school or kindergarten. Nothing took place by accident.

Every decision was geared for the individual's needs— "What is best for *this* boy in *this* situation? When is the right time for *him* to step out?" There are no pat formulas. Every child is different and will thus require a different timetable.

Every decision in our family is approached in this manner. We, as parents, control the environment the boys are exposed to. We kept guns from our boys' range of playthings long beyond when other parents would buy such toys. We did not keep guns, murder, cruelty and death under cover forever, but *we*—not playmates or the Sunday school toy box—determined when these concepts were to be introduced. We also carefully select everything they watch on TV. There are too many wrong values communicated through television for a Christian parent to be unconcerned about what is watched.

We have certain friends whom we believe possess certain tremendous qualities. We lose no opportunity to thrust our boys into their presence and thus be exposed to those qualities.

There come times as a child grows when he needs to practice, to feel the "tug" of the world, to learn how as a

Christian to resist it. *You* should control when this happens. This is *not* overprotection. You are simply expanding his boundaries and environment at the pace *you* deem best. Do so wisely; let him go when he will profit from it, but protect him when he is endangered.

Because we maintained this policy, our sons, in their early years, were highly vulnerable. They were more prone to be hurt and to be exploited by other children. They have not learned to fight for their rights or to boldly assert themselves. But Judy and I are traveling the same road with them. We often have to spend time together trying to piece together some meaning out of a difficult situation which the boys are having to cope with.

Though their progress in the "ways of the world" is perhaps slower than usual, the benefits of early teaching of values and attitudes is beginning to pay off as they grow. Now that their values and attitudes are reasonably solid, their growth is accelerating rapidly and will probably surpass that of their peers. They have learned early to walk a different path. Resisting the false values of the world will be quite natural as they face increasingly greater conflicts.

All this requires great time and energy, but that's the price of success. You must evaluate every relationship, every situation, every influence and decide how it will contribute to your ultimate goals for your child. Half-hearted measures will never work. The opposition is too strong. You must wage vigorous daily combat on your child's behalf.

Decision-Making Skills

In today's *now*-oriented society, you are one of the few people in your child's life who will consider his *future*. Few other people will teach him foresight and eternal perspectives.

By the time your child leaves home, he will be solely accountable for everything in his own life. He must know how to make decisions. It is your job to slowly transfer that responsibility onto his shoulders. If you wait with transferring that responsibility until the moment he leaves home, the burden will crush him. His lack of practice leaves him unable to handle it.

Accustom him to responsibility as he grows by carefully giving more latitude in his decisions. The more he learns to do, the greater his abilities. The more responsibility he receives, the more he is capable of making decisions. A growing youngster needs to be faced with choices that will affect him personally. A teen-ager needs the recognition that his own decisions carry more weight. A youth has the right to become an adult, and no parent should impede the process. If a young adult is going to capably decide about his education, vocation, marriage, finances and church involvements, he must receive much practice in decision-making.

A toddler, for instance, can be faced with simple choices: whether to have a snack of dried figs or peaches; a ten-year-old can decide between two TV programs; a high school junior can decide between going on a weekend ski trip with the youth group or a business trip with Dad. Decisions must not be too heavy too soon, but the older a child grows the greater number of decisions he should make regarding his own life. You are training a future twenty-year-old to exercise full control. Providing early decision-making opportunities prepares him. Prayerfully you must give choices that carry greater consequences. If he makes an unwise choice now, you are still with him to help. When he is an adult, he will have to make correct choices, for there will be no one to lean on.

As you give increased freedom in decision-making, you are widening his boundaries. As the "rope" is let out, he knows you are there to protect him if there is danger or uncertainty. He experiences great freedom when allowed to develop in such security.

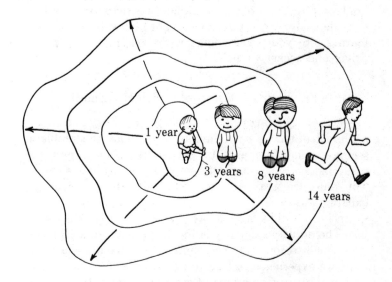

As a child matures, his boundaries widen
and his environment expands.

Practical Skills

A child needs to confront tasks and thus acquire skills in
order to function capably as an adult. A perceptive parent
sparks motivation through his own enthusiasm. He includes his child in his activities, jobs, errands, hobbies and
recreation. He allows him to participate as he repairs,
builds, shops, cleans, and plays.

As early as possible include your child in your activities
(a clever parent can find things for even a two-year-old to
do). He will enjoy his learning and will, through the years,

acquire proficiency through having been included by an interested and encouraging parent. A toddler may just stand, hold your tools, and ask a million questions. But by the time he is sixteen, if you have taught him well, he may be tearing into your car's engine while *you* hold the screwdriver and socket wrench.

Prepare Your Child to Cope with His Emotions

A child often faces emotional stress. It is easy to dismiss a child's dilemma as unimportant because the problem seems so small from an adult perspective. Though perhaps meaningless to us, the matter may be shattering to a child. You must learn to *feel* with your child the emotions he experiences.

Inside a child's mind a vast emotional network is forming. The adult personality is the accumulation of all life's experiences recorded in the mind. The impact of the emotions we experience is hard to gauge. It is so well hidden. The majority of emotions affect the personality in ways that even a child's parents are unaware of.

Joy Wilt identifies ten traumas that plague children the most and can adversely affect their emotions: separation from parents, nightmares, moving to a new neighborhood or school or church, the addition of a new family member, visits to the doctor, dentist or hospital, death, divorce, injury, adoption, and sexual offenses.[12]

Emotions can be totally illogical. If a child *feels* rejected or abandoned even though there has been no *actual* rejection (you are leaving him for only an hour), his subconscious can convince him that he has been rejected or abandoned permanently. Even imaginary sensations can generate intense emotions—trying to reason with a five-year-old boy that *there are no lions* in the attic! I did this with my boys. They *knew* there were no lions, but that didn't keep their hearts from pounding when I turned off the light and went downstairs.

Children can confound our finest efforts. They can go through life accumulating guilt and inferiority for no reason. Parents make it worse with criticism and demands for perfection. Even when a youngster appears normal and well balanced, anger or self-condemnation can fester beneath which will gradually turn him into a Jekyll-Hyde personality.

Such emotional turbulence can go undetected until much later. During his teen years, a decade of masked feelings may suddenly erupt in hostile rebellion. In his mid-thirties he may suffer an emotional breakdown. Repressed emotions are volatile.

It is possible, however, to minimize the potential emotional hurts your child experiences. You can deflect harmful input and keep it from penetrating into your child's subconscious.

Emotions trapped beneath the surface of your child's mind will not go away on their own. They resemble trapped gasses below the earth's surface which must somehow find release. The longer they are repressed, the more they will seethe and boil and the more likely that they will erupt as an emotional Mount St. Helens. You can insure that your child's emotions do find proper ventilation. When emotional bubbles are able to rise to the surface and escape, usually their negative effects can be dissipated. The secret of giving your child emotional wholeness, then, is to draw his emotions to the surface.

Several techniques can help you accomplish this. Most importantly, help your child identify and reveal his feelings. Freely discuss how he feels. Communicate acceptance and approval. By advising, "You *should* feel such-and-such. . .," when he doesn't, you lay the groundwork for guilt. He needs to learn that it's all right to feel sad, lonely, depressed, or angry, that it's fine to cry. He needs to hear about *your* emotions.

Emotions are a puzzle for a tender youngster. He needs to learn how they work, and your own openness will help tremendously. He must learn to look within himself and know what he is feeling and why. When you know a certain trauma is coming (from an anticipated move, for example), you can prepare him. Emotional surprises are more devastating than emotions we've prepared for.

If your youngster knows you understand, love, and accept him no matter what he is feeling, much of his pain will be alleviated. Expression of emotions is probably the finest psychological therapy in the world. Let him receive healing through your listening ear and tender heart.

Physical activities release huge quantities of emotional energy. Children express themselves as they yell, laugh, tumble, run, swing, jump, and climb. These activities can "uncork" much tension and frustration. Being cooped up in clean clothes stifles something that aches to get out. A parent who puts his child in such a predicament invites trouble. Children need to be rambunctious and noisy, to get dirty and sweaty from hard play. Even teen-agers and adults require physical exercise to vent emotional pressures.

A young child who has undergone a particulary traumatic incident can be helped by re-enacting it. A psychiatrist often has his patient talk about and re-experience a given moment of pain. Re-living it forces the supressed emotions to the surface. A parent can use the same technique with a child who has had a painful experience. Much of the debilitating energy can be vented by having him talk about what happened and then having him act it out with his siblings, making a game of it. Soon the whole thing becomes associated with laughter and play. The painful memory—because it has been exposed—is then far less hurtful. In our family we have acted out dog bites, bee stings, bad dreams, and scary stories, all with great success. By all sharing the experience we are able to reduce the pain that has been felt.

We are often afraid of things we don't understand. Most children feel things far more deeply than they can understand. They can often be afraid of nothing but the emotions welling up from within. They have never before experienced guilt, lonelines, or insecurity. They don't know what to expect. They can't even form words to talk about what's eating away inside.

One of the prime benefits, therefore, of identifying and discussing emotions is that a youngster comes to know himself more deeply. With that understanding comes confidence and strength. As you help him to grapple with his fears, frustrations, joys, and the unique traits of his own temperament, his fragile self-esteem will be strengthened.

In our home we discuss emotions like we discuss the weather. They're always "up front and right on the table" where we can all "see" them. Judy and I make a point of saying, "Tell us what you're feeling." Then we teach our sons how emotions function and how to handle them.

Part of this training involves teaching the proper methods for venting certain emotions. While having a certain feeling may be perfectly acceptable, often the behavior associated with it is not.

If Robin comes and says, "I'm mad at Gregory and I feel like clobbering him!" we thank him for revealing his feelings to us.

Then we devise some alternative method for dealing with the frustration. It might be time for a solo game of tetherball, some pounding with a hammer and nails, or a half-mile run with Dad. But we are always glad for the honest expression and release of what was felt. Children need to know and recognize their feelings, to openly discuss them, and to learn how to deal constructively with them.

The stresses of each age are unique, but the teen years and early twenties provide a mountain of them. Growing from adolescence into adulthood is a demanding and painful process. One of the most significant things you can do to ease your child through this time is to prepare him early for the tensions he will face. (If you're uncertain about this, consult James Dobson's *Preparing for Adolescence*.)

All adolescents wrestle with peer pressure, competition, fatigue, physical changes, schoolwork, failure, decisions about the future, questions about sex, misgivings about self-worth. Enable yours to cope by offering wholehearted acceptance and by helping him develop the capacity to deal with emotions.

And as he reaches the age where spiritual questions and doubts are an issue, you must remember what it was like when *you* were in the same situation. Face these issues on *his level*, not on a spiritualized plane. During these years of struggle a young person needs a strong, mature, sensitive parent who can question with him, cry with him, and listen to him. He needs a parent who will teach him to know himself, to pray, and to discover answers.

Prepare Your Child to Cope with the World's Value System

A hundred years ago if you had faithfully taught your children the tenets of the Christian faith, chances are they would have accepted your faith as their own. Today, however, children are rampantly rejecting the beliefs of their parents.

Today's children are not inherently more rebellious than their predecessors—children have always been rebellious. Something more fundamental is at work in our generation which most Christian parents are at a loss to understand. But any parent who seriously desires to provide his child a Christian basis for life *must* understand this change. Otherwise he will be unable to instill Christian values in the child.

What has caused this problem? There has been a drastic change in the way the world looks at truth. There have been changes in every generation, of course, but they have been nothing like the fundamental change that has taken place in our own time.

Throughout the history of western civilization, man has reasoned on the basis of absolutes. There was an absolute true and it was opposed by an absolute false. This foundation came from Christianity, which views God as the absolute truth and the absolute good. Anything contrary to God's principles is false and therefore wrong. God's laws are considered good, right, and true—their opposites are not.

Though everyone was not a Christian, nevertheless this "Christian" way of approaching things influenced everyone. Men disagreed about what the absolutes were, about which things were right and which were wrong. But they all held the underlying assumption that absolutes did in fact exist. If something was wrong, it was wrong! Someone may have chosen to disagree about whether it was in fact wrong. Another may have chosen to do it even though it was wrong. But few would have argued, "It may be wrong for you but right for me." Something couldn't be *both* right and wrong at the same time.

All this has now changed. The world has come to accept a point of view, based not on opposites and absolutes, but on *relativism*. Opposites are no longer necessarily opposite—good is not necessarily opposite from bad, truth is not necessarily opposite from falsehood; opposites can *both* be true depending on your viewpoint. One thing can be right for me and the same thing can be wrong for you, and vice versa. All is relative to the perspective one chooses to adopt.

This is particularly significant for Christian parents. Your child will be bombarded with relativistic points of view in school, from friends and from the media. If you become aware of this problem, you may even notice relativistic tendencies in your church and in your own thought patterns. We all have been subtly affected by it.

Since you are raising your child with the basic premise that certain things *are* right and others *are* wrong, and that God *does* hold us accountable, your child often will find himself in a conflict. If you consider the enormous amount of time he will spend away from home, it is easy to see why he can be confused about values when he reaches high school and college where the world's ideas are highly persuasive.

You must, as a parent, come to an understanding of these changes that have taken place. Then you must instill in your child an awareness of the irreconcilable differences between the Christian viewpoint and the world's viewpoint. You will have to study and read in order to be adequately informed. You must alert yourself to these dangers because you are your child's spiritual guardian. He is extremely vulnerable. The world's net is closing in to entangle your family. Equip yourself to recognize its deceptions. You may have to terminate relationships which are destructive. You should discuss with your child the sort of philosophies he is encountering in school. You will have to screen TV programs, books, magazines, and movies. You will have to firmly impart absolutes and teach him to recognize relativistic thinking. Only then will your child have the intellectual capability to perceive and apply the truth.

Preparation for the World's Demise

I view the future in the light of biblical prophecy. I realize therefore that I must provide my children with a spiritual foundation for a day that is surely coming soon—a day in which they could witness and experience deprivation, persecution, and even martyrdom as Christians.

Admittedly it is difficult to imagine what sort of life my children may face. In the relative comfort and ease of the free West, it is easy to gloss over the words of men like Lindsey, Wilkerson, Solzhenitsyn and Wurmbrand—men who declare that a drastically different day is coming to the West, a day when many of our present freedoms will be gone, a day of suffering and persecution.

As I jog around our neighborhood in the early morning before most households are stirring, I often think, "These houses seem so tranquil. Maybe all this gloomy preoccupation with the future is nothing but hollow fear. Maybe our American way of life will simply continue as it has for years. Maybe my boys *will* grow up to enjoy a normal middle-class life."

But as I think further I have to admit that I'd have had the same thoughts in 1929 or in 1937. Everything would have appeared peaceful enough. But doom, crisis, death, war, and poverty would have been lurking everywhere.

No, the forces that mold and shape history do not begin on tranquil streets but originate on much higher planes. All about me, once the restful homes awaken and bustle with life, I see indications, however slight, of Satan's strategy to wrest control of the world from the hand of God and to take the souls of my sons from His hands.

A war is going on!

I continually remind myself that the relative harmony I feel when playing on our lawn with my children is not a true measure of the state of the world. If it were late 1939 and we were playing in a village five miles from the English Channel, it would be difficult to forget. The distant rumble of machinery, planes, and guns would have constantly reminded me of the world's real condition. My heart would pound as I kept myself ready to sweep my sons into my arms and whisk them away to safety.

But today there are no sounds of planes, bombs, or mortar shells. We are easily lulled to sleep. But these are foreboding times. When I hear someone say, "Isn't it exciting to be living in the last days?" I wonder if "exciting" is the right word. Knowing that my sons could be martyred before they reach my age sobers me.

"How can I prepare these boys for the things they may someday face?" I ask myself. "These are the sons God has given me. I have them for a few brief years to prepare them. They could be part of God's army that will one day face the might of Satan himself. An ordinary, 'Smile! God loves you!' faith will do them little good when that day comes."

My children, and yours, are called to be valiant soldiers for God. As anything less they will be unable to serve and lead God's people in their generation. God has given us, their parents, the gigantic responsibility to mold them into people who will be able to do anything He asks of them.

Only God knows what my family and I might face together. In a moment of trial the effectiveness of my preparation will face the test of fire. I hope my boys can look into my face in that moment and see a reflection of the love of God. And I hope I will look into their faces and see angels smiling.

I have rarely been so sobered as when I read the following account. It hit me so hard because I realized the day could come when God would also require such courage of me, my wife, and my sons. Whether it be in a cold dark prison, in a furious storm, in a bloody war, or as Satan unleashes his wrath upon us, it's for such a day I am preparing my family.

When George Jaeger took his three sons and his elderly father out on the Atlantic Ocean for a fishing trip, he had no premonition of the horror that he would face in a matter of hours. Before he would step on shore again, Jaeger would watch each son and then his father die, victims of exhaustion and lungs filled with water.

The boat's engine had stalled in the late afternoon. While increasing winds had whipped the sea into great waves, the boat rolled helpless in the water and then began to list dangerously. When it became apparent that they were sinking, the five Jaeger men put on the life vests, tied themselves together with a rope, and slipped into the water. It was 6:30 p.m. when the sinking craft disappeared and the swimmers set out to work their way toward shore.

Six-foot waves and a strong current made the swimming almost impossible. First one boy, and then another—and another. . . swallowed too much water. Helpless, George Jaeger watched his sons and then his father die. Eight hours later, he staggered onto the shore, still pulling the rope that bound the bodies of the other four to him.

"I realized they were all dead—my three boys and my father—but I guess I didn't want to accept it, so I kept swimming all night long," he told reporters. "My youngest boy, Clifford, was the first to go. *I had always taught our children not to fear death* because it was being with Jesus Christ. Before he died I heard him say, 'I'd rather be with Jesus than go on fighting.' "

Performance under stress is one test of effective leadership. It may also be the proof of accomplishment when it comes to evaluating the quality of a father. In that awful Atlantic night, George Jaeger had a chance to see his three sons summon every ounce of courage and self-control he had tried to build into them. The beautiful way they died said something about the kind of father George Jaeger had been for fifteen years.

Few fathers will have their leadership-effectiveness tested so dramatically or so suddenly. For most men, the test will come in small doses over a long period of living. But the test comes to all, and sooner or later the judgment is rendered. . . . All five people in that dangerous situation required every bit of strength derived from the relationships they had forged over the years.[13]

The Lord may not so dramatically test the effectiveness of my leadership. But in the uncertain times ahead I consider the likelihood to be very strong.

"The test comes to all, and sooner or later the judgment is rendered."

"But, Lord," I sigh, "I could never face that. I love my boys too much."

"But I love them too," He responds, "even more than you do. I gave them to you. I placed the vision for their lives in your heart. And remember, I lost a Son myself, for the good of others. I may call upon you to do the same. I love you and I love your sons, more than you can fathom. The days ahead are perilous times that will require sacrifice and giving. You may be chosen to drink of the same cup of sorrow that I had to drink when I gave up my only Son. If you are so chosen, drink the cup with courage, as my servant George Jaeger did."

One day my sons, my wife and I could stand side-by-side before a firing squad because we profess Jesus as our Lord. I want to be able to say, "I have prepared my sons for this." Even if my youngest were only ten, in that moment God would call him to be a man.

The nurturing of that manhood is presently in my hands.

Notes

1. Marguerite Kelly and Elia Parsons, *The Mother's Almanac.* Garden City, NJ, Doubleday, 1975, p. 179.
2. Ibid., p. 179.
3. Ibid., p. 149.
4. James Mallory, *The King and I.* Wheaton, IL, Scripture Press, 1973, pp. 156-157.
5. Larry Christenson, *The Christian Family.* Minneapolis, Bethany Fellowship, 1970, p. 86.
6. Don Highlander, *Positive Parenting.* Waco, TX, Word, 1980, p. 46.
7. Ibid., pp. 25-27, 161.
8. Kelly and Parsons, p. 177.
9. Larry Christenson, p. 93.
10. Bill Gothard, "Ten Steps Toward Corrective Discipline," Institute in Basic Youth Conflicts, adaptation by the author.
11. Haim Ginott, *Between Parent and Child.* New York, Avon, 1969, p. 87.
12. Joy Wilt, *Happily Ever After.* Waco, TX, Word, 1977, chapts. 11 and 12.
13. Gordon MacDonald, *The Effective Father.* Wheaton, IL, Tyndale House, 1976, pp. 13-15.